Congressional Elections

Politics and Public Policy Series

Advisory Editor

Robert L. Peabody

Johns Hopkins University

Congressional Elections

Barbara Hinckley
University of Wisconsin
Madison

Congressional Quarterly Press
a division of
CONGRESSIONAL QUARTERLY INC.
1414 22nd Street N.W., Washington, D.C. 20037

Printed in the United States of America

Second Printing

Library of Congress Cataloging in Publication Data

Hinckley, Barbara, 1937-
    Congressional elections.

    Bibliography: p.
    Includes index.
    1. United States. Congress — Elections. 2. Elections — United States. 3. Voting — United States. I. Title.

JK1967.H55   324.973   81-2413
ISBN 0-87187-171-8   AACR2

Foreword

Congressional Elections, by Professor Barbara Hinckley of the University of Wisconsin-Madison, is an important synthesis of a burgeoning new field of electoral research. For more than four decades, political scientists, historians, and journalists have focused on presidential elections almost to the neglect of congressional contests. Voting results for presidential elections were easier to obtain, less messy to analyze and interpret. Even such a pioneering study as *Congressmen and the Electorate* (1966), by Milton C. Cummings, Jr., concentrated upon the interrelationship between the vote for president and the vote for congressmen in presidential-election years.

During the late 1960s and 1970s, interest in congressional elections as a research focus began to expand. In 1978, the creation and funding of the Committee for Congressional Election Research, based at the Michigan Center for Political Studies, led to a dramatic upsurge in research and writing on congressional elections. Barbara Hinckley, who served as a member of that committee, provides in this book the first comprehensive overview of the past literature together with innovative analysis of the 1978 and earlier congressional elections.

Every two years, the decisions made by the electorates for one-third of the Senate seats and in all 435 House districts have critical consequences for representative government in the United States. First, at the individual level, primary and general election results advance or set back the careers of some 1,000 party politicians—about 100 candidates for the Senate and another 900 or more men and women aspiring to seats in the House. Among the winners will be a few destined for congressional or national leadership, perhaps even the presidency.

Second, the aggregate outcome of seats won and lost determines which congressional party will achieve a majority in the House and Senate, with the obligation to organize those bodies. The results of the 1980 congressional elections, for example, led to a divided Congress: a Senate controlled by Republicans for the first time since 1954; a House still in the hands of the Democratic party.

Third, the size of the respective majorities in the House and Senate goes a long way toward determining the success or failure of the president's legislative program and the future electoral hopes of his party. Historically, voters have seldom elected a president of one party without also electing a House of Representatives controlled by the same party. Increasingly, in the second half of the twentieth century—1956, 1968, 1972, and now, 1980—Republican presidents have had to contend with Democratic majorities in the House.

After establishing a framework for analyzing congressional elections, the author takes an intensive look at the voters and how they receive and process information about the candidates and the issues. Chapters 3 and 4 discuss the powerful impact of incumbency on elections as well as the more amorphous influences of party. In Chapters 5 and 6, the candidates and the issues come under more detailed examination. Chapter 7 treats one of the most fascinating but least understood facets of congressional elections—the similarities and differences between congressional races in midterm and presidential-election years. In the concluding chapter, Professor Hinckley explores the policy and research implications of her subject.

Educated at Mount Holyoke College and Cornell University (where she received her Ph.D. in 1968), the author has maintained a keen interest in electoral politics. She is the author or editor of many books and more than a dozen scholarly articles. Since 1972, she has taught political science at the University of Wisconsin-Madison.

Heretofore, most of our knowledge about how voters select leaders in the United States has been limited to the selection of presidents. By concentrating on House and Senate races, *Congressional Elections* fills an important gap in electoral studies.

Robert L. Peabody

Preface

This book brings together and extends what is essentially a new research undertaking—the study of congressional elections. In the past, political scientists, like journalists and citizens, paid little attention to congressional races. Studies of congressional voting were primarily adjuncts of presidential voting studies. Basic data were unavailable; entire subject areas remained unexplored. Recently, however, there has been a marked upsurge in congressional election research. New data have been provided by the 1978 National Election Study and have led to a number of conference papers and journal articles. Other data-collection projects are now under way. The time should be right, then, for a first full analysis and accounting of the subject.

Congressional Elections combines the results of past studies with some original unpublished analysis. It covers major topics already being investigated: incumbency, party voting, the effects of issues, candidates, and presidential voting. At the same time, it supplies a framework to interrelate and make sense of the separate findings. Voting models drawn from presidential elections take information as given: there is competition between two candidates who are known to the voters. But in voting beyond the presidential contest, such information cannot be assumed. People must first decide what information they need before they can make any voting decision. Moreover, the kind of voting decision will vary depending on the information available. The emphasis on information—and not competition—can help explain the major findings reported and provides a base for studying the wide range of American elections.

The results of the study provide a comprehensive examination of the influences at work in congressional elections. They should be of value to undergraduates, graduate students, and scholars in tracing what we know and do not know about the subject. They also can serve to challenge some of the conventional wisdom—about the reasons for House incumbents' electoral success, the decline of party voting, and the effects of the presidential vote in congressional elections. The book reflects not only the excitement of a new research enterprise, but also its frustration. There are many areas about which there is little to say. We know much more about the voters than the candidates or other relevant political actors. The recruitment of candidates, primary elections, the effects of the campaign, the impact of party or nonparty groups remain to be studied. The book, therefore, should be taken as a first study and base for further work—to be added to and revised as the work progresses.

I wish to acknowledge some unusual good fortune in the people and circumstances contributing to the study. Colleagues in the congressional election field shared with me their ideas and work in progress. My experience on the Committee for Congressional Election Research was invaluable in exploring the potential and limits of the 1978 survey design. A graduate seminar in congressional elections at the University of Wisconsin generated some major ideas and arguments as well as several independent research projects. Lee C. Shapiro spent a long, often thankless semester on basic information-gathering essential to the book. I was particularly fortunate in readers Robert Erikson, Glenn Parker, and Lyn Ragsdale for their serious review of the manuscript and important suggestions. I was also particularly fortunate in the help of Congressional Quarterly staff, and especially Barbara de Boinville, in extending, correcting, and updating the information in the tables and appendices. Few authors find a publisher already knowledgeable in the subject matter of the study. Finally, I wish to thank editor Jean Woy, who insisted that there be a book on congressional elections and lent her considerable expertise at all stages of the process to make it a reality.

Barbara Hinckley

Contents

Figures and Tables

1

A Framework for Analyzing Congressional Elections

Congress, by constitutional provision and twentieth-century practice, shares with the executive the job of governing the nation. The president sends a bill to Congress, but a congressional committee decides whether to consider the bill. It is the committee's bill—not the president's—that is debated on the floor. The president, working through the Office of Management and Budget, sets the overall priorities for government spending and sends a detailed budget to Congress. But Congress has its own priorities, and the House and Senate appropriations committees can raise, lower, or ignore any White House budget request. The president is chief executive of an immense government bureaucracy, and yet many bureaucrats have closer ties to Congress than to the chief. Key committee members can reinstate or cut an agency's funding, threaten an investigation or other unpleasantness, and can continue to do so long after even a two-term president has come and gone.

In times of critical decision, Congress decides whether to accede to the president or to raise its own constitutional voice. "Fine," said Congress in 1950 in Korea and 1964 in Vietnam: of course we will support the president and do what he asks. "Wait a minute," said Congress in 1969: we'd better reconsider that 1964 decision.[1] "No," said Congress in 1919 and 1920: America will not join the League of Nations nor sign the Treaty of Versailles; we, the United States Congress, will make the nation's foreign policy on that question. Beyond the critical decisions and the front-page news—in all the matters that never reach the White House—Congress goes on with its business of governing. Crop subsidies and the price of food, tariff restrictions and tax loopholes, government contracts to private industry, oversight of the Food and

1

Drug Administration or the CIA—all are a part of congressional business.

Moreover, the particular membership elected to Congress makes a difference in these decisions. Committee leadership is based on seniority, and seniority requires being re-elected. Hence the defeat of one key senior member can change the course and outcome of a committee decision. The question of whether more Republicans or Democrats are elected determines which party will organize the House and Senate, chair the committees (deciding between the most senior committee Republican and the most senior committee Democrat), vote the staff allotment, and decide other rules. The ratio of Democrats to Republicans elected is reflected in the party ratios of most of the committees. Presidential leadership in Congress is inhibited or enhanced depending on whether or not the president's party has a majority in the House and Senate.

Although party lines in Congress are often blurred, Democrats and Republicans will tend to vote differently on a wide range of issues. Issues concerning welfare, education, labor, foreign aid, and fiscal policy have typically found a majority of Democrats voting against a majority of Republicans on the roll calls. The antiwar votes in Congress in 1969 and 1970 also found Democrats and Republicans opposing each other as did the Senate's 1978 vote on the equal rights amendment. The Senate voted 54-44 in favor of the equal rights amendment (specifically, to extend the time period permissible for states to ratify the ERA). But if the vote had occurred only one year later, following the 1978 election and the defeat of a few liberal Democrats, the results would probably have been reversed.

In 1980, the presidential election so preoccupied media attention that it was difficult to find even minimal congressional election coverage. But when the smoke had cleared after the election, seven liberal Senate Democrats were defeated and replaced by some very conservative Republicans, and the Senate majority had edged over to the Republican side. (See Appendix Table A-2 on page 144.) The leadership, all committee chairs, and the results of Senate roll call votes would change accordingly.

At the individual level, too, elections make a difference. They can defeat influential leaders—a Birch Bayh or George McGovern or Edward Brooke—and raise others to influence through repeated re-election. Wisconsin voters brought Republican Senator Joseph McCarthy to the Senate and kept him there, and on his death replaced him with Democratic Senator William Proxmire, who continued to be re-elected. The two senators, poles apart on issues, style, and approach to government, made their own impact on the nation's policy through the process of elections.

Nevertheless, while the American public elects both a president and members of Congress to carry on the governing activity, only one-half of that process has been studied intensively. In the literature on elections, the "American voter" is a presidential voter. Most of what we know about party attachment, issue voting, or citizen participation has developed primarily from the presidential contest. Indeed, even when congressional elections are studied, as we will see later in Chapter 7, they can become merely a kind of presidential popularity poll—less of intrinsic interest than for what they say about the president. The classic study *The American Voter,* published in 1960, initiated two decades of electoral research. As the authors stated explicitly at the beginning of the volume, it was "a study of voting in presidential elections."[2] The work following that study has kept the same focus of attention.

This past emphasis on presidential elections is quite understandable. It accords with the traditional perception of American government as presidential government. If the president, as symbolic leader of the nation, is seen as "in control" of all matters of government,[3] then attention might well be focused on that election. It also accords with the availability of electoral data. In the past, the survey results considered so important in election research have been widely available only for presidential voting. Their expense has restricted their use at the state and district levels where senators and representatives are elected, while the national sample surveys have asked few questions on congressional races. Yet if elections are important to national government, both elected branches must be studied. And if voters are important for political scientists to study, then they must be studied beyond the one most visible and possibly atypical contest.

The American voter, in short, is not merely a presidential voter. In fact, it can be contended that we know very little about voting behavior, or the influences on this behavior, until we look past the presidential election. This book, therefore, will venture beyond the presidential contest to a study of congressional elections. Interest in this subject has recently increased, and various studies of congressional voting have been undertaken. These studies need to be integrated and extended. Major patterns can be identified. Problems can be raised for future research. In addition, in the process of learning more about congressional voting, we should come to see more clearly the larger range and implications of all American voting behavior and the very different contexts of influence within which it occurs.

THE SEVERAL DIMENSIONS OF ELECTORAL ACTIVITY

To citizens of a democracy, elections are familiar and frequently occurring events. The newspapers supply a continuing commentary on elections past and elections to come. Schoolchildren hold elections in their classes, and adults choose club or organization officers. But what is an election, and how can it be studied? What distinct components of an election need to be identified and combined? The very familiarity of the activity may lead us to think that we know more about elections than we do.

First, it is important to see the multidimensional nature of electoral activity. An election implies both individual choice and a collective event. To elect, according to *Webster's New Collegiate Dictionary,* is "to select by vote for an office, position, or membership." Individuals *vote,* but voters together *elect.* In other words, two selection processes are occurring simultaneously. At the individual level, there is a cognitive process: individuals think about the choice and make a decision. At the collective level, there is a counting or aggregative process—an adding together of the individual decisions. The voters together select the candidates for office, but this need not mean that they have "decided" something or engaged in any collective cognitive activity. Collectivities, especially as large as thousands of voters, rarely "think," "decide," or "speak." On the other hand, a lopsided electoral margin for one candidate over another need not mean that most individuals have thought the same things. In analyzing elections we need to exercise caution when moving from one selection process to the other.

In addition, an election implies a translation of information from one sphere of activity to another. Individuals use information to make a decision, but much of the information is provided and shaped by a larger political context. The candidates are recruited. Endorsements and newspaper space are allocated. Campaign strategies are designed. Past events are known and affect present choices. All of this may be seen as electoral activity, but it is distinct from the activity of the individual voter. Voters select, interpret, search for, or screen out this activity for their own activity of voting. Hence what goes out from a campaign headquarters is not necessarily what is received by the voters. What voters perceive is not necessarily what candidates do. Again, we need caution in moving from one electoral activity to the other—from the voters to the political context and back to the voters.

Elections, then, both *aggregate* and *translate* activity at one point and on one level to another. A diagram of these processes is shown in Figure 1-1. Elections translate political events to individual perceptions and back to political events: i.e., the election result. And they aggregate the individual decisions into a collective event. Indeed, here we can see their claim to importance in democratic government: they connect the political context with the individual citizen, and the individual citizen with the collective result. They are a way, literally, of making one's vote "count."

Figure 1-1   The Several Dimensions of Electoral Activity

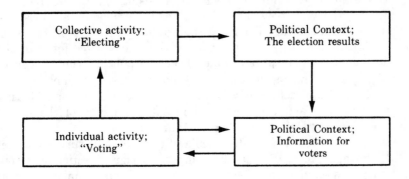

NOTE: The arrows in the diagram show the direction of electoral activity. Thus, individual voters receive information from the political context but also actively seek and select information from it.

This multidimensional view of elections can supply perspective on some of the continuing controversies and problems of analysis. One may, for convenience, decide to focus on one particular portion of electoral activity as opposed to others. Some people study individual perceptions with the use of survey data. Some look for patterns in the aggregate voting results. Some pay more and some less attention to the political context within which the voting occurs. Each mode of study can have value in supplying information otherwise unobtainable, so long as it is recognized that each is only a part of the larger phenomenon to be explained. Elections, as Figure 1-1 illustrates, cannot be reduced to only one level or one sphere of activity.

The figure also clarifies the strengths and weaknesses of the various kinds of data used in studying elections. These data can be broadly classified as *survey data, aggregate voting results,* and *contextual data.* Surveys ask a sample of people, so selected as to represent the full population being studied,[4] about their political attitudes and behavior. They concentrate on the activity of voting (the lower left-hand corner of the figure). Aggregate voting data concentrate on the election results (the top half of the figure). People study the vote margin received by candidates, from reported election statistics, or the change and patterns in results across a number of races or across time. Contextual data focus on the activities of candidates and others that are presumed to affect the results (the right-hand portion of the figure, especially the lower right-hand corner). People study campaign spending, media coverage and treatment, or the activities of candidates already elected to office.

Each of these kinds of data has its own contribution to make and its own limits in explaining election results.

Survey data provide a means of focusing on the individual's cognitive activity. Surveys have asked people, among other questions, about their perceptions of parties, candidates, and issues in the campaign. Since the surveys also ask people whom they voted for or intend to vote for, these perceptions gained from the political context can be linked to the voting result. Surveys, therefore, have the advantage of getting to the individual level where the voting actually occurs. This is a major advantage and can help explain the popularity of the survey approach in recent electoral research. Surveys have the disadvantage, however, of expense and limited availability. A reliable survey requires great care and preparation in the sampling design, questionnaire construction, and quality control for the interviews. Professional expertise is required. One does not merely conduct one's own telephone poll or hire professionals to do it—at least not without a large grant in hand for the funding. In general, researchers must rely on the few major survey operations and their selection of questions and question wording. Survey data are limited also in their dependence on what the respondents to the questionnaire can or wish to say. A person who flipped a coin in the voting booth may be unlikely to admit this to the interviewer. Consciously or unconsciously, people rationalize their attitudes and behavior. Hence some of the answers may have only limited value for any explanation.

For example, the turnout actually recorded in elections across the country is always lower than the turnout reported in surveys. People evidently see voting as a citizen duty and a good thing to do and are hesitant to admit that they did not vote. In 1978, according to the actual turnout figures, 35 percent of the eligible electorate voted, but about 45 percent of a national sample surveyed said that they voted. The same tendency to make one's attitudes and behavior seem better and more coherent than they are might be expected on a number of other survey questions.

With aggregate data we find the strengths and weaknesses reversed. Aggregate data are widely available from volumes of election results, census information about the states and counties voting, and other compilations. Unlike survey data research, aggregate data information can be gathered on one's own, utilizing only library resources. These results also have the advantage of being "hard" data: they are factual. In contrast to the "soft" survey data of perceptions and interpretations, they are events that have occurred and can be verified. Aggregate data have the disadvantage, however, of not being able to get to the individual level for the votes that they seek to explain. For example, using aggregate data we may find that a House candidate ran unusually well in all blue-collar areas of a district, but we do not know whether people voted for the candidate because they found this socioeconomic factor important or for some other related or peripheral issue. Perhaps the blue-collar areas were also Italian and there was an ethnic issue in the campaign, or perhaps the non-blue collar families in those districts voted even *more* heavily for the candidate, in which case the vote would have nothing to do with the socioeconomic status of the voters.

To pursue the question, we would want data at least on (1) the voters' own socioeconomic status (as they perceived it); (2) their perception of the issues important in the campaign; and (3) their vote. Of course, this information also has limits. People might not know their socioeconomic status or rationalize their reason for the vote. An Italian voter may have hated the Irish candidate, but the ethnic issue may not come across in the survey. We might find instead that the voter liked the other candidate's "experience," or "past voting record," or felt that it was "time for a change."

The third kind of information, contextual data, has been less frequently utilized in elections research. It offers the important advantage of getting beyond the voter to the rest of the political world where electoral decisions are made. A candidate's decision to run, a campaign strategy, the success of money raising, key endorsements—all may be decisive to an election. The voters merely respond to the influences and decisions shaped elsewhere. Indeed, the study of elections has often been criticized for staying within the very confined "black box" of individual voting behavior. (This is presumably the box in the lower left-hand corner of Figure 1-1.) It has been difficult, however, to collect contextual data systematically. It is one thing for the press to speculate or campaigners to assert that this or that issue or strategy or contribution made a difference. Maybe they are right, and maybe they are wrong. It is quite another problem—and a much more difficult one—to measure campaign emphasis or media coverage or a pattern of endorsements.

Later chapters will report some important beginning efforts; nevertheless, in the past at least, this difficulty in data collection and measurement has posed a major limit on the contextual data approach. Like the aggregate analysis, this approach, too, must confront the problem of linkage with individual voters' perceptions. What is sent out from a campaign—or from any other point in the political context—may not be received by the voters. To return to that blue-collar race, the losing (Irish) candidate may claim that it was the winner's money, targeted in blue-collar areas, that made the difference. The winner may claim that it was the emphasis on inflation as an issue and the slogan "It's Time for a Change." Unless we can link events in the political context to the perceptions of voters, we may merely be substituting one black box for another.

As Figure 1-1 makes clear, each of these approaches is potentially important. Future chapters will explore more fully their strengths and limits in congressional elections research.

VOTER AND POLITICAL CONTEXT: THE PROBLEM OF INFORMATION

Recognizing the several dimensions of electoral activity directs attention to the problem of transferring information from one dimension to another: most critically, to the voter's problem in selecting information from the political context. What can be assumed about the way voters choose information and about the kinds of information made available to choose? And what does this mean for the way people are selected for office in American government?

According to the traditional democratic view of elections, voters choose among candidates on matters important to them. These may include questions of policy (a candidate's stand on inflation or abortion), questions of qualifications (a candidate's experience or perceived trustworthiness), or some combination. So, voters confront a choice, select and interpret information for the choice, and balance the many and possibly contradictory questions to reach a decision. The candidate selected thus represents the collective choice of the people—the adding together and balancing of all those individual thoughtful decisions.

Nevertheless, as many writers point out, this traditional view may not be realistic. Human beings, voters included, will balance the costs of making a decision against the expected benefits from making a correct one (or the expected losses from making an incorrect one).[5] Costs include time, energy, and other resources spent in gaining information about the candidates. For many citizens, voting decisions are not very important. People do not care greatly about the outcome, or they feel that their one vote will not make a difference. They may have decided to vote because it is their duty as citizens, because it is fun to do on election day, or because they are in the polling booth to vote for another office. But given the low expected benefits, the costs spent on making the decision will also be low. Voters may choose the easiest, most obvious, or most generally reliable means of making their decisions.

Indeed, these citizens appear to be the more typical, not the deviant cases, among the public.[6] Generally, public interest in and information about politics is low. The voters themselves constitute only about one-half of the eligible electorate or less, depending on the office being voted for. In the 1972, 1976, and 1980 presidential elections, an average of 54.1 percent of the estimated population of voting age actually voted; in the off-year congressional contests, 36.2 percent voted in 1974 and 35.2 percent in 1978. (See Appendix Table A-1 on page 143.) In recent years, approximately 50 percent or slightly less have voted in presidential elections, and about 40 percent or less have voted in the off year when there is no presidential contest. The turnout for primaries or special elections held at other times is lower still. When one moves beyond turnout to more demanding political activity, such as attending political meetings or talking with others about the election, the proportion of interested citizens drops drastically. Also, as we will see in Chapter 2, when one moves beyond the presidential election to other elections, citizen interest and information drop even further. Many people have not paid much attention to the congressional campaigns and admit they "did not care much" about the outcome.

In short, people are many things besides citizens. They are individuals, family members, workers, members of informal social groups. They have many decisions to make and to gain information about, and politics may not be high in their order of priorities. People are also many things besides decisionmakers. Much of their time may be spent following routine, not thinking, or evading or ignoring the need to make a decision.

This point is particularly important for studying nonpresidential elections. Many of the current models of voting behavior appear to be thinking, unintentionally, of a presidential contest. These studies assume that *the indifferent citizen does not vote.*[7] With very little or no opinion or information about the candidates, the rational citizen, it can be argued, would not spend the resources necessary to go to the polls and vote. But in the real world of American elections, many contests occur simultaneously. A voter might not be indifferent to the presidential outcome, but virtually indifferent to who wins the race for the House, the state senator, the various judgeships, and the coroner. Given the simultaneity of American elections, the thinking of the almost completely indifferent voter must be considered, and models excluding this indifference may be applicable only to a very narrow range of elections.

Some people, of course, are keenly political. They enjoy competition or are concerned about issues and actively seek all available information in a campaign. Some races will produce much more information than others: the costs of gaining information will be lower. To take the obvious case, information is so widely available in presidential campaigns that it might be difficult to *avoid* learning something about the contest. Almost all voters could report having "some contact" with the candidates. In congressional races, by contrast, voters need to spend much more of their resources to gain information. On some occasions, the information may seem so clear—a widely reported scandal, an obvious and critical difference between the candidates—that the voters' task of decisionmaking is an easy one.[8] At times, information may be abundantly provided or actively sought, but it need not be this way. As we move beyond the study of presidential elections—and the voting models drawn from these studies—we need a view of the selection process that can accommodate this variety.

THE SELECTION PROCESS

As a first step toward such analysis, consider, from the standpoint of common sense and experience, how people make selections. They must, for example, buy a soap or hire someone to fill a position. If they have the time and consider the outcome important, they can compare the merits of the various competitors: the soaps' prices, ability to clean, or availability in a range of bathroom colors; the job applicants' past experience, recommendations, or personal impressions. However, they can save time and effort, under the pressure of other decisions, by adopting a general and easy rule to follow in all such situations involving choice. They almost always buy the product lowest in price or hire the job applicant with a particular educational record. They save even more time and effort if they select a general rule so that no real choice even confronts them: they buy the soap they have bought before or hire the candidate already in the firm and in line for the position.

Two critical steps in this process of selection can be usefully distinguished. First, by evaluating the information available and the importance of the selection, one decides the rule: whether to apply the specific information one has available, or to apply a general rule requiring no further specific information, or to search further for information. Second, one applies the rule selected to make the actual decision. In effect, then, there are two "decisions": the first concerns how one will make the decision—the decision about the decision—and the second concerns the selection itself.

Figure 1-2 outlines this two-step selection process for the individual voters (the solid lines in the figure) and the influences from the political context (the broken lines). Depending on the importance and the information available, voters may decide to engage in a *general-choice* or a *specific-choice* decision. If they like the incumbent (i.e., the candidate in office at the time of the election) and know nothing about the challenger, then, like the buyers of soap, they may choose the candidate they have chosen before. Partisanship offers another general rule for making electoral decisions. One may not know both candidates or either candidate but decide that Democrats generally can represent one's position better than Republicans. Other general rules can be suggested. Under some circumstances, voters may decide to toss the rascals out— the rascals being all incumbents or all Democrats or Republicans. Alternatively, given sufficient information, voters may weigh the specific merits raised by the candidates and issues in the campaign. The

Figure 1-2   The Two-Part Selection Process

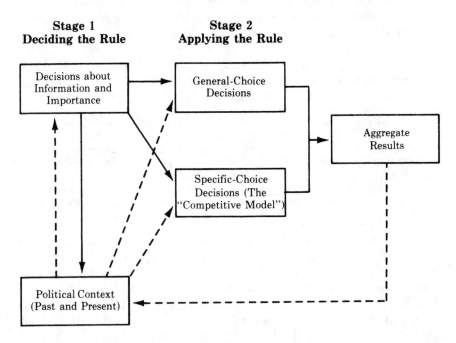

NOTE: The solid lines indicate choices by the individual voters, and the broken lines indicate the information from the political context.

consideration may be short or extended. The differences between the candidates may be obvious, or the situation may require an even further search for information. This specific-choice decision, or "Competitive Model," represents the traditional view of all voters' activity.

Information from the political context also affects these decisions, as indicated by the broken lines in Figure 1-2. The political context, past and present, affects the information available as well as the general- or specific-choice decisions. The quality of the candidates who run and the visibility of the race can help decide the answer to the first-stage question. Take a race with a Senate incumbent seen to be in trouble and a former governor persuaded to enter the contest as challenger. The contest is widely reported by the news media and both candidates campaign vigorously. The context affects the voters' perceptions that, yes, specific information is available to make a decision. In contrast, in other races perhaps the former governor does not run, or perhaps a candidate not predicted to run well is not given much coverage. The political context also affects the general- and the specific-choice decisions. A national issue may hurt the reputation of one political party or alienate a large group of previously affiliated voters. A scandal involving the incumbent can force voters to apply other general rules (for example, voting against people involved in scandals) or to search for further information about the challenger. In each of these cases, the context affects the voters' decisions.

We can compare this framework with other current accounts of how voters make selections. According to Stanley Kelley and Thad Mirer, people can follow very simple decision rules in the act of voting:

> The voter canvasses his likes and dislikes of the leading candidates and major parties involved in an election. Weighing each like and dislike equally, he votes for the candidate toward whom he has the greatest net number of favorable attitudes, if there is such a candidate. If no candidate has such an advantage, the voter votes consistently with his party affiliation, if he has one. If his attitudes do not incline him toward one candidate more than toward another, and if he does not identify with one of the major parties, the voter reaches a null decision.[9]

There are two decision rules in the Kelley-Mirer model. The major rule requires a weighing of preferences between the candidates and parties. The second rule—voting with one's own party affiliation—is applied only if the first does not produce a decision. If neither rule suggests a choice, the person does not vote. The authors tested this model for four presidential elections and reported very good results. A similar model is suggested by Richard Brody. In this case, people simply weigh their preferences for the two candidates and reach their decision; or, if no candidate is preferred, they follow their party affiliation. If neither a candidate preference nor a party affiliation helps make the selection, a person does not vote.[10]

The models, it should be clear, suggest ways of formalizing the ideas of traditional democratic theory about voting. They are also ways of explaining what we have called the specific-choice, or Competitive Model, decisions. Note that both models take information about candidates as given: it is available to voters in applying the decision rules. Both also appear to equate the decision to vote in an election with the decision to vote for one contest. Both discussions, in fact, seem to be thinking about presidential elections. In other elections beyond the presidential level, the models may be less useful in explaining the results—if information is not available for two candidates, or if people who turn out to vote for one contest stay to vote for others. Modifications would seem necessary in applying these models beyond the presidential level.

In contrast, the selection process outlined in Figure 1-2 *specifies a separate and prior calculation of the costs required in making one kind of decision as opposed to another.* There is a prior decision about the decision: i.e., whether to apply a general rule or to apply the kind of specific-choice decision outlined by Brody or by Kelley and Mirer. Depending on the information available and the importance attributed to the outcome, people may decide to make such a specific choice or not to do so. At times, then, they may vote for the candidate known and thought well enough of (although not preferred), or they may use party affiliation as the primary, and not secondary, rule of decision. Elections can be expected to differ in the amount of information available and in the importance people attribute to the outcome. Thus to explain voting behavior, we need some prior decision rules about which particular decision rules will be applied.

This two-part view of the selection process makes sense in terms of the individuals who actually do the voting: it allows voting to be seen in perspective with all other selections people are called upon to make. It links the individuals to the political context—including both present and past results. It also links the individual voters with the collective results by focusing on the general influences confronting all voters. Party, incumbency, the candidates recruited, the issues of the campaign—all can be identified and used to explain election results. Figure 1-2, therefore, represents an extension and elaboration of Figure 1-1. Information becomes the critical link between voter and political context, given the multidimensional nature of elections. But since information cannot be assumed as readily available, people must first decide what information is to be sought or applied before any actual voting decision can occur.

This view of elections also accommodates the variety of voters and races. People deeply concerned about issues will always make specific-choice decisions; others are typically general-choice "party" voters. Some races, such as the presidential contest, will automatically provide more information than others. In voting for coroner, few people may weigh the merits of the particular candidates, while many may do so for president. Therefore, the framework used here for congressional races could be applied more generally to all elections.

Finally, this selection process will provide some unifying explanation for material to be considered in the following chapters. Each chapter addresses one key influence already identified as important in congressional elections: incumbency, party, the candidates, the issues, the effects of presidential voting. Three of these influences—party, candidates, and issues—are also important to presidential elections; the other two are contributions from the congressional research. This format allows a comprehensive account of the congressional elections literature, with its major findings, key arguments, and unresolved questions. But the literature cannot tell us why these influences are important or why some are more important than others, nor can it relate the findings of one chapter to those of another. It cannot say, for example, why incumbency and party together can explain a major portion of the congressional vote, why incumbency is more important in House than in Senate races, or why very few congressional candidates, even the losing candidates, are negatively perceived by voters. The framework being offered here can provide such explanations by focusing on the different decisions possible given different kinds of information. Given the preliminary state of the research, no fully satisfactory accounting is possible. Nevertheless, the framework should provide a beginning explanation both within and across chapters.

Every second year, in even numbered years, on the first Tuesday after the first Monday in November, American voters elect all 435 members of the House of Representatives and one-third of the Senate (senators being elected for six-year terms). At the same time, the voters may be selecting candidates for governor and many other offices; in every other election (every four years), they are selecting candidates for president. The congressional members thus elected will fill the committees, pass the legislation or decide not to pass it, oversee the bureaucratic agencies or decide to leave them alone, and say to a wide range of questions on American national government "Yes," "No," or "Maybe next year." It is a major job that these applicants are being selected for. Examining how they are selected and the critical influences on their selection will be pursued in the following chapters.

NOTES

1. Congress supported President Harry S. Truman's decision to ask the United Nations to intervene in Korea and President Lyndon Baines Johnson's decision to increase American military involvement in Vietnam. The Tonkin Gulf Resolution, passed in 1964 to support the increased military effort, was later repealed by Congress following the growing criticism of the Vietnam war.
2. Angus Campbell et al., *The American Voter* (New York: John Wiley & Sons, 1960), p. 7.
3. This is part of the "cult of the Presidency" well described by Thomas Cronin in *The State of the Presidency,* 2nd ed. (Boston: Little, Brown & Co., 1980), pp. 75-118. See also Fred Greenstein, "What the President Means to Americans," in *Choosing the President,* ed. James D. Barber (Englewood Cliffs, N.J.: Prentice-Hall, 1974), pp. 121-148.
4. Sampling theory is based on probability theory. In drawing a sample, each person in a population (for example, eligible voters in a congressional district or nation; or a particular subset of these citizens) is given an equal, or at least known, probability of being selected for the sample. Thus, in a properly drawn sample, one can infer from the sample statements about the population as a whole. One can also state the range of expected error and the confidence one can have in the results. For example, a particular sample might have a 3 to 4 percent sampling error, meaning that most of the time (say, 95 percent of the time) the sample results will be within 3 or 4

percentage points of the results if one were to survey the population as a whole. Great increases in sample size will produce small reductions in sample error; thus one has to calculate the most economical sample size for the desired results. Most of the major surveys cited in this study would report a sampling error between 3 and 5 percentage points. In other words, a figure reported as 46 percent of the sample could range between 42 and 50 percent of the population.

5. See, for example, Anthony Downs, *An Economic Theory of Democracy* (New York: Harper & Row, 1957); Gordon Tullock, *Toward a Mathematics of Politics* (Ann Arbor: University of Michigan Press, 1968); William Riker and Peter Ordeshook, "A Theory of the Calculus of Voting," *American Political Science Review* (March 1968): 25-42; Michael Shapiro, "Rational Political Man: A Synthesis of Economic and Social Psychological Perspectives," *American Political Science Review* (December 1969): 1106-1119; Otto Davis et al., "An Expository Development of a Mathematical Model of the Electoral Process," *American Political Science Review* (June 1970): 426-446; and John Ferejohn and Morris Fiorina, "The Paradox of Not Voting: A Decision Theoretic Analysis," *American Political Science Review* (June 1974): 525-536. A good review of the literature is provided in Richard Niemi and Herbert Weisberg, eds., *Controversies in American Voting Behavior* (San Francisco: W. H. Freeman & Co., 1976), pp. 22-31.

6. For studies of participation, see Sidney Verba and Norman Nie, *Participation in America* (New York: Harper & Row, 1972); Campbell et al., *The American Voter;* and Norman Nie et al., *The Changing American Voter* (Cambridge: Harvard University Press, 1979). A good discussion of the information costs in voting is provided by Downs, *An Economic Theory of Democracy,* chaps. 11 and 12.

7. See Downs, *An Economic Theory of Democracy,* chap. 13.

8. See V. O. Key, Jr., *The Responsible Electorate* (Cambridge: Harvard University Press, 1966).

9. Stanley Kelley, Jr. and Thad Mirer, "The Simple Act of Voting," *American Political Science Review* (June 1974): 574. See also their note 7 indicating other decision rules that might be applicable.

10. Richard Brody, "Communications," *American Political Science Review* (September 1976): 924-926; and Brody and Benjamin Page, "Indifference, Alienation and Rational Decision," *Public Choice* (1973): 1-17.

2

Voters and the Context of Information

Information is shaped by and selected from influences in the political context. This information in turn will affect the kind of decision rule selected and the subsequent decision made. At the outset, then, we need to understand the voters' information about congressional races and examine how this is affected by such influences as the type of race, the kind of candidate, and the amount of resources spent on the campaign.

We know from public opinion studies that *interest* and *information* vary with education and socioeconomic situation. The higher their educational level, the more people are likely to be interested in and informed about politics. Groups most disadvantaged in American society—by race, occupation, and background situation—are least likely to be informed, to join in political action, or to make their preferences known at the polls. Interest and information also vary with personal self-esteem and a sense of "political efficacy"—the sense that one can have an impact on government and that people in office care what one thinks. Of course, those lowest in education and in other socioeconomic characteristics also tend to be lowest in self-esteem and efficacy. The migrant worker and the unemployed eighteen-year-old, not very well-stocked with self-esteem at the moment, might answer quite realistically: no, they do not feel that their personal views have any real impact on decisionmaking in government; no, people in government do not care what they think.

The present analysis assumes that variation in interest and information and goes on to ask what other factors are important. Generally high-information voters may have more or less information in particular races and under particular circumstances, and the same is true for low-information voters. It is these more particular influences, arising from the political context, that will be examined.

INTEREST AND INFORMATION AMONG VOTERS

While public interest in politics is generally low, it is considerably lower in congressional than in presidential elections. This fact can be seen at both aggregate and individual levels and has been documented throughout 20 years of electoral research. Studies from the 1950s showed that a low proportion of House voters had "read or heard anything" about the candidates.[1] In the 1970s, people could say where they themselves stood on the Vietnam war and other major issues of the day and on a general liberal-to-conservative ideological rating. They could say where the presidential candidates stood and where the parties stood, but they could not place the House candidates, even when the incumbent's position was available from the record and the party of the candidate was supplied.[2] When people were asked open-ended questions about what they liked and disliked about the candidates for president, governor, and senator, most (87 percent) could make at least two comments about the two presidential candidates, while 64 percent could do so for governor, and barely half (52 percent) for U.S. senator.[3] By 1978, most people could recognize the names of a number of would-be presidential candidates and rate how they felt about them, whereas less than half could recognize and rate the two House candidates in their own districts, even when the names of these candidates were supplied.[4]

In a 1978 national survey, for example, only 49 percent of the voters in contested House elections reported having "any contact" with or "learning anything about" the two candidates contesting the election.[5] Note, first, that having any contact does not demand very much in terms of information gathering: to say yes to the question, people could have heard or read something about the candidates, seen a campaign flyer, or received any of a variety of kinds of contact. Note, also, that self-reported contact, like turnout, may be higher than actual contact. Since contact can also be considered a citizen duty and a good thing to do, the survey figure may exaggerate the amount of contact occurring. Note, finally, that these are the voters only—those interested enough to vote in an off-year election. So, following the traditional democratic view of elections, if one expects voters to select and weigh information about both candidates competing in a race, less than half would qualify even by this minimum measure.

These results can be evaluated against the two-part selection process outlined in Chapter 1. If there are two candidates in a race, and people have not "read or heard anything" about at least one of them or cannot recognize their names when supplied with them, any specific-choice decision is impossible. The Competitive Model will not be useful in explaining these decisions.

Some interest, we can assume, is necessary to gain and select information. The contrast in interest between presidential and congressional races can be seen by the pattern of House voting turnout in presidential-year and off-year elections. (See Figure 2-1 on page 20.) In presidential election years, House voting is very close to levels of presidential voting: most people who go to the polls to vote for president also vote for a House candidate. In the off years, by contrast, turnout drops sharply. This regular zigzag pattern has held across all twentieth-century elections. The same contrast in interest is sharply outlined in the survey results of Table 2-1. Although approximately two-thirds of the people questioned cared about the presidential race and paid some attention to it, approximately two-thirds did not care about or pay attention to the House race in their district. However, the proportions who *voted* in these two contests are almost the same. A large number of people who did not care much about the congressional race and paid little or no attention to it still managed to vote in the contest. How they voted in this situation becomes a key question to be examined.

Table 2-1 Electing the President and Congress: Concern, Attention, and Voting Participation, 1972 (Percentage of Sample, N=841)

	Vote for President	*Vote for Congress*
Concern[1]		
Cared great deal	62.8	38.5
Not very much or none	37.2	61.5
Attention[2]		
High	71.5	35.4
Low	28.6	64.6
Voting Participation		
Voted	72.1	67.4
Did not vote	27.9	32.5

[1] "Generally speaking, would you say you personally cared a great deal which candidate won the presidential election (seat in the U.S. Congress) this fall, or that you didn't care very much who won?" The 8%, for both president and Congress, who answered "some" were included in the low concern category. "Don't knows" (2% for each) were also categorized as low concern.

[2] "Would you say you followed the presidential campaign (campaign in this district for the U.S. House of Representatives) with a great deal of attention, moderate attention, not very much attention, or that you really didn't follow the presidential (congressional) campaign at all?" "Great deal" and "moderate" responses were categorized as high attention. "Don't knows" (0.4 and 0.5%) were included in the low attention category.

SOURCE: Barbara Hinckley, "Issues, Information Costs, and Congressional Elections," *American Politics Quarterly* (April 1976): 131-152. By permission of the Publisher, Sage Publications, Inc.

Figure 2-1 Turnout for House Elections, 1952-1980

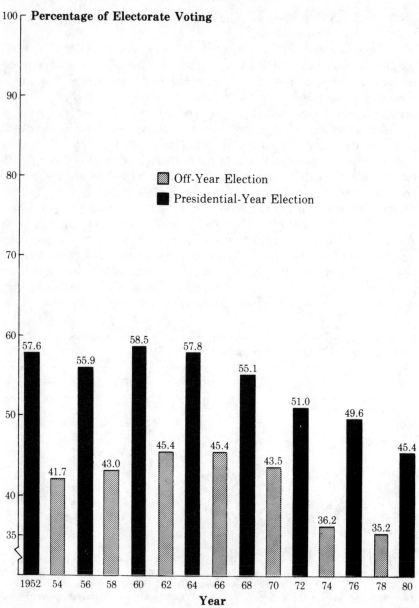

100 ┌ **Percentage of Electorate Voting**

SOURCE: Bureau of the Census, *Statistical Abstract of the United States,* 1979, p. 513. The 1980 percent of electorate voting was calculated by the Census Bureau, which used the unofficial 1980 vote returns in *Congressional Quarterly Weekly Report,* November 8, 1980, pp. 3299, 3338-3345. Votes cast for all of the minor parties and votes for unopposed candidates were not included in their tally. The estimated population of voting age for 1980 does not reflect 1980 census figures.

FACTORS AFFECTING INFORMATION

There are differences, however, in interest and information found within congressional contests: most notably, between House and Senate, and between races with and without incumbents contesting. One rough measure of information is the traditional "name recall" question: people are asked immediately after an election if they know the names of the candidates in the race. Admittedly something of a memory test also, the question has been asked repeatedly since 1952 for a number of offices. As Table 2-2 makes clear, the same pattern has held across a 20-year period. Virtually everyone can name the presidential candidate. Many can name the gubernatorial candidate, fewer the Senate candidate, and fewest of all the House candidate.

The table also shows an increase over time in the proportion of people able to supply the candidate's name. By the end of the two decades, House voters' recognition was about where Senate voters' recognition was 20 years before. Either information or memories appear to have improved over time. But the major results are clear. Candidate recognition varies with the office contested. Senate candidates fare

Table 2-2   Voter Recognition of Candidates for Office, 1952-1972

| | *Percentage of Voters Able to Name the Candidate They Voted For* | | | |
	President	Governor	U.S. Senator	U.S. Representative
1952	100	73	60	45
1954	*	*	*	*
1956	100	*	50	33
1958		81	53	49
1960	100	*	55	48
1962		*	*	54
1964	100	78	63	47
1966		85	78	65
1968	99	82	72	60
1970		91	79	55
1972	99	94	79	55

* Data not available.

SOURCE: Gary Jacobson, *Money in Congressional Elections* (New Haven: Yale University Press, 1980), p. 12. © 1980 by Yale University Press. Reprinted by permission. Data provided by the national election studies of the Survey Research Center, Center for Political Studies, University of Michigan.

poorly compared to the other candidates for state-wide office but do well compared to House candidates. Table 2-2 depicts the results for voters only. Information levels would be lower if nonvoters were included.

Some new work shows even more clearly the House-Senate differences in information. After the 1978 election, a national sample was asked a number of questions on the congressional races that had just occurred. Respondents were supplied with the names of the candidates in their own states and districts and asked, if they recognized these people, to rate how they felt about them on a "feeling thermometer" scale from 0 degrees (most negative) to 100 degrees (most positive). Note that the question taps the kind of cognitive activity actually demanded in the voting booth: there, too, people have the names supplied and are asked to recognize and rate the candidates. Respondents were also asked whether they had had "contact with" or "learned anything about" the candidates and, if so, to check the kinds of contact from a list provided. The results are shown in Table 2-3 for House and Senate and for races where incumbents ran against challengers and where nonincumbents ran against each other. Again, the results are shown for voters only.

Table 2-3 presents very clearly the voters' low information about House challengers. Most voters could recognize and rate the incumbents—both Senate and House—and the Senate challengers, while less than half could recognize and rate the House challengers. Moreover, comparing challengers with the other nonincumbents, Senate challengers are like the other candidates in recognition, and House challengers are not. While 78 and 70 percent respectively recognize House Democratic and House Republican nonincumbents, only 44 percent recognize the House challenger. The same pattern is seen in the contact questions. In sharp contrast to the contact with all other candidates, less than half of the voters said that they had any contact with or learned anything about the House challenger.[6]

Therefore, in Senate races in 1978, one could say that the minimum conditions for choice between candidates were present. The voters could report some contact with both candidates in the race and could recognize their names and rate them. These conditions hold both for the races with incumbents and for the open-seat races where nonincumbents compete against each other. In the House open-seat races, information is less, but still considerable. However, in the House races where incumbents run against challengers—and these are by far the most frequent in occurrence—the conditions for choice are not present. Voters know the incumbent, but less than half know the challenger who runs against the incumbent. Both recognition and contact, as we will see later, affect the voting results. Being recognized, when the other candidate is not recognized, is a decided electoral advantage.

Other House-Senate differences are observable from Table 2-3. Senate voters overall exhibit more information, more media contact

Table 2-3 Name Recognition and Contact in the House and Senate

Percentage of Voters

Voters Who Could Recognize and Rate the Candidates[1]

	House		Senate	
	N		N	
Incumbents	(757)	92	(395)	95
Challengers	(757)	44	(395)	85
Nonincumbents D	(116)	78	(150)	93
Nonincumbents R	(116)	70	(150)	83

Voters Who Had Contact with the Candidates[2]

	House					Senate				
	N	Any	Met	Read About	TV	N	Any	Met	Read About	TV
Incumbents	(575)	94	23	74	52	(395)	97	9	75	83
Challengers	(757)	46	4	34	22	(395)	85	5	65	73
Nonincumbents D	(116)	81	18	61	51	(150)	95	12	85	85
Nonincumbents R	(116)	72	11	58	50	(150)	91	7	79	79

[1] Respondents were supplied with the names of candidates in their own states and districts and asked, if they recognized the names, to rate them from zero to 100 degrees on the feeling thermometer. A small number who said yes they could recognize the candidates' names then said no they could not rate them. The measure reported here is based on those who could both recognize and rate.

[2] Respondents were asked, among other questions, if they had had any contact with the candidates, had met them personally, read about them in newspapers or magazines, or seen them on television. The fact that the same percentages are given for nonincumbents in the last two columns of the table is apparently a coincidence of the data and not an inaccuracy in reporting.

NOTE: These results are based on voters in contested elections in 1978. The term incumbent includes only those running for re-election, and nonincumbent refers only to those nonincumbents running against other nonincumbents, i.e., for open seats.

with candidates—especially from television—and more information about open-seat contests. Indeed, the open-seat candidates do as well or better than incumbents in contacting voters. House incumbents, as might be expected, show higher levels of personal contact.

At this point it is worth asking whether the competitiveness of the race affects voters' interest and information. If voters know there will be no contest or a lopsided one, their interest and efforts at information gathering may be reduced. Some preliminary evidence from 1978 suggests a negative answer. Voters reported caring about the outcome of the House race and following the 1978 campaigns in about equal proportions regardless of whether they faced (1) a contest with an incumbent running, (2) an open-seat race, (3) a totally uncontested election, or (4) a contested one. Approximately the same proportions reported voting in the House race in all contested elections, in contests with incumbents, and in open-seat races. House voting was lower, as would be expected, in the uncontested elections.[7]

Further work is needed on how the competitiveness of the race affects voters' interest and information, and later chapters will consider this question. Nevertheless, these first indications are suggestive. Although House voters show similar amounts of *general* interest and concern in races with and without incumbents, they are much more likely to have information about the two competing candidates in the open-seat race compared to the race between the incumbent and the challenger.

In some House races, of course, the challengers are known and can mount active and victorious campaigns against incumbents. A study based on district polls in the 1974 and 1976 elections supplies a number of illustrations. Recognition of serious and active challengers rises in the course of a campaign: one challenger, in fact, increased his recognition rate (i.e., the percent who could recognize the candidate's name) by 55 percentage points in a six-month period.[8] Moreover, candidates succeed in getting across to voters in other ways besides recognition. The case is cited of a Republican challenger who had run two years before against the same incumbent and only narrowly lost. Both times, the challenger campaigned on the importance of change and the need for congressional reform, while the incumbent countered with an attack on the qualifications and personal characteristics of the challenger. A survey conducted before the election indicated that this campaign information had indeed been received. At least people agreed that the Democrat was "more qualified to hold public office" and that the Republican challenger "would try hardest to reform Congress."[9] All challengers are not unknowns. Some—from previous election tries, the extent of campaign activity, or other qualifications—can get across to voters much more than others.

Information About Incumbents and Challengers

We can look more closely at those incumbents and challengers so differently perceived by voters. House elections "are won in the off year," said political scientist Charles Jones as long ago as 1966.[10] Being in Congress amounts to a continuing campaign. Incumbents enjoy the material support that comes from the job and the perquisites of office. These include the franking privilege that allows free mailing to constituents and local news media, the paid staff for Washington and district offices, the distribution of government publications, and an allowance for visits to the district. Incumbents can use the job itself to campaign for re-election. They perform constituency service—supplying information and interceding with the bureaucracy for people back home.[11] They can claim credit for government projects in their district and other government decisions. In general, according to David Mayhew, they can use the job for "advertising," "credit claiming," and "position taking," all of which can help maintain a very visible and positive reputation with their constituents.[12] Moreover, there is evidence that incumbents work hard at maintaining this reputation—in their number of visits home[13] and through their skill at building a "home style" and presenting themselves and government issues to their home constituency.[14]

In a 1980 newsletter, a Maryland congressman courts his constituents by asking:

"When is the Metro subway line opening to the stations at White Flint, Twinbrook, Rockville and Shady Grove?" That's one of the most frequently-asked questions I hear from residents in communities along the Wisconsin Avenue/Rockville Pike corridor in Montgomery County. . . .[15]

The newsletter goes on to report the representative's continuing concern for this important policy problem and shows him, in hard hat, inspecting the construction. While we do not think of the House of Representatives as centrally involved in subway construction, the incumbent is expressing his concern for the district and its people. He is representing them. We can multiply this by all the incumbents and their various and particular district concerns to see how simply being in office helps return them to office.

It is important to note that incumbents achieve more than visibility in their newsletters, district visits, and other expressions of constituency concern. Incumbents are perceived *positively*, and these positive perceptions, as we will see later, are more important in explaining the vote than mere recognition. Senate incumbents also enjoy office support and can advertise, claim credit, and take positions. Yet, Senate incumbents do not obscure the voters' perception of challengers, nor do these incumbents enjoy the re-election success of their House counterparts.

Some recognition may be a necessary condition for achieving electoral success, but it is not a sufficient one.

Who are the candidates opposing these formidable incumbents? They appear on the whole, if one looks at the aggregate results, particularly unlikely to achieve electoral success. In 1978, for example, in 309 House contests between incumbents and challengers, 249 or 81 percent of the challengers had held no previous elected office. They compiled on the average 34.3 percent of the vote in districts that had given their party's candidates 35.3 percent of the vote two years before. Whereas the average House candidate (including incumbents, challengers, and open-seat candidates) spent $112,000 on the campaign, the average challenger spent $72,000.[16] The 1978 House spending figures break down as follows:

Mean Dollars Spent

	Democrats		Republicans	
	N		N	
Incumbents	(200)	$111,424	(109)	$138,765
Challengers	(109)	70,947	(200)	73,043
Open-Seat Candidates	(52)	212,671	(52)	192,514

These figures show the same pattern that has held since 1972 when spending data could first be collected.[17] Open-seat candidates lead in spending, followed by incumbents, followed by challengers.[18] In 1978, the open-seat nonincumbents outspent the challenger nonincumbents by almost 3 to 1.

The different qualifications of these various incumbents and challengers may also affect recognition. Simply by dividing some particular candidate qualifications into two categories—those expected (1) to help or (2) not to help challengers—we can see if challengers are significantly more likely to be recognized and voted for in the first category as opposed to the second. In other words, are challengers who have run for Congress before more likely to be recognized by the voters than challengers who have not run? Are challengers facing relatively new incumbents more likely to be recognized than those facing senior incumbents? Table 2-4 summarizes the results for candidates included in the 1978 survey. "Yes" is recorded if the qualification listed made a significant difference to the challenger's recognition and vote.

According to the results, challengers increase their recognition when they have run for Congress before, engaged in relatively high campaign spending, and face relatively new and nonentrenched incumbents. Past elective office, however, does not make a difference. Challengers who have run before are recognized by 61.0 percent of the voters, while challengers who have not run are recognized by 42.1 percent. Challeng-

Table 2-4   Effects of Candidate Qualifications on Recognition and the Vote

Candidate Qualification	*Effect on Challenger*	
	Recognition	Vote
Challenger's Experience (past congressional race or not)	Yes	Yes
Challenger's Experience (past elective office or not)[1]	—	—
Challenger's Spending (Jacobson measure)[2]	Yes	Yes
Incumbent's Seniority (first term or more senior)	—	—
Incumbent's Seniority (first and second term or more senior)	Yes	Yes
Incumbent's Past Safeness (won previous election by less than 55 percent of the vote or safer)	Yes	Yes
Incumbent's Past Safeness (won previous election by less than 60 percent of the vote or safer)	Yes	Yes

[1] Includes past U.S. representative and all elective state, county, and local offices.

[2] See Gary Jacobson, "Congressional Elections, 1978: The Case of the Vanishing Challengers," *Sage Electoral Studies Yearbook,* vol. 6, ed. L. Sandy Maisel and Joseph Cooper (Beverly Hills: Sage Publications, 1981). Jacobson uses a slightly different recognition measure, but he reports that the results are similar no matter which recognition measure is used.

NOTE: All results except for challenger spending are computed by the author from data in the 1978 National Election Study, Center for Political Studies, University of Michigan. The measure of recognition follows the discussion and results reported in Table 2-3. A "Yes" is reported when the relationship achieves a significance level of .05 or lower, based on chi square results with one degree of freedom. In other words, there would be a 5% or less chance of achieving the particular results by chance.

ers who run against incumbents winning their previous election by less than 60 percent of the vote are recognized by 60.5 percent of the voters, while those who run against safer incumbents are recognized by 33.1 percent. In the even more marginal races (where incumbents have won previously by less than 55 percent of the vote), challengers increase their recognition. In the most marginal races they are recognized by 64.3 percent of the voters and in all other races by 39.1 percent. All of the qualifications affecting recognition also make a difference to the vote.

"For he that hath, to him shall be given."[19] The biblical observation is nicely illustrated by House elections. We can now begin to see the complex of factors that helps incumbents and contributes to the invisibility of challengers. By being safe, well-known, and able to create a positive impression by all their work in Congress and all their visits home, incumbents can discourage strong challengers from entering the race and soliciting funds for what looks like a losing cause. All of these factors in turn affect the challengers' recognition and electoral success, and so incumbents are returned to office and the process is repeated. Although these factors, themselves interrelated, will need further disentangling, two points are worth emphasizing from this first analysis. Candidate qualifications do affect the information voters use in making a selection. And from the standpoint of House challengers, things are not totally grim. Challengers can get across to voters under some conditions. Moreover, some of these conditions are under the challengers' control.

Effects of Campaign Spending

Campaign spending has long been thought critical in supplying information to voters. Certainly, by the efforts made to raise money and the amount of money spent, the candidates themselves have believed its importance. However, not until after the campaign finance reforms of the 1970s could the effects of money be systematically investigated.

Table 2-5   Average Campaign Expenditures, 1972-1978 (In Thousands of Dollars)

	Incumbents		Challengers		Open-Seat Candidates	
	D	R	D	R	D	R
House						
1972	49.2	52.3	30.2	32.3	96.8	91.4
1974	46.3	81.4	59.3	20.7	103.1	79.9
1976	79.1	90.2	44.6	55.5	144.1	97.7
1978	111.4	138.8	70.9	73.0	212.7	192.5
Senate						
1972	381.1	559.7	205.7	312.4	481.2	460.2
1974	562.5	600.4	390.3	284.5	531.6	273.6
1976	555.9	800.3	645.5	349.0	636.3	877.6
1978	594.2	2065.7	830.3	552.0	808.9	812.8

SOURCE: Gary Jacobson, *Money in Congressional Elections* (New Haven: Yale University Press, 1980), pp. 53, 54, and 228. ⊙ 1980 by Yale University Press. Reprinted by permission.

NOTE: Includes only those candidates with major party opposition.

Before that time, no comprehensive data on contributions and expenditures were available. Despite the enormous spending in congressional campaigns, no one knew if it helped, who it helped, or how, specifically, it worked in the process of selection.

Recent studies of congressional campaign spending can begin to answer these questions. First, it becomes clear that money helps some candidates more than others. As we might predict from the preceding discussion, spending is particularly important for nonincumbents and especially challengers. It significantly increases recognition and affects the vote.[20] *Spending does not help incumbents.* Indeed, if one looks only at the summary results, it would seem that the more incumbents spend the worse they do. These summary results, however, hide the fact that incumbents' spending tends to be reactive: it increases or decreases in response to the spending of the challenger. Thus the incumbents opposed by the most serious challengers would spend more than other incumbents and would do less well at the polls. Controlling for this interactive effect, we find that incumbents' spending makes little difference to their recognition or the vote.[21] In other words, facing the same level of opposition from challengers, incumbents could spend a lot or a little money and find scant difference in the results. Challengers, on the other hand, improve their recognition and chance for election with each increment of money spent. These findings hold for the Senate and House: spending helps the challenger much more than the incumbent. Table 2-5 shows spending for incumbents, challengers, and open-seat candidates.

Of course, recognition, probability of success, and the availability of money to spend are all highly interconnected. When these components are separated,[22] spending appears to have its major effect on increasing the recognition of the least visible candidates. These candidates can then campaign more equally with the more visible candidates in making their qualifications and positions known to the voters.

Money buys attention—not votes. It is worth noting that the four House challengers who spent more than $400,000 in the 1978 campaign all lost the election, exactly like so many of the thriftier and more indigent candidates who were also challengers. But they lost it narrowly, averaging 47 percent of the vote.[23] The voters still preferred the incumbents, but they appeared to be aware that there were two candidates to choose from and a choice to be made.

It follows that campaign contributors can have their greatest impact on electoral outcomes by giving to the challenger's campaign, and yet few contributors follow this route. Party committees support incumbents more than challengers as do the individual contributors and the nonparty political action committees (PACs).[24] While there is much debate on the impact of political action committees on elections, their effects appear similar to other observed effects in the advantage to incumbents.

In 1976 and 1978 House races, Democratic party committees spent 64 percent of their funds for incumbents; the 72 top business PACs spent 67 percent (heavily but not exclusively for Republicans); and the 43 top labor PACs spent 68 percent for incumbents (heavily but not exclusively for Democrats). The Republican party committees spent less on incumbents (36 percent), but they had fewer incumbents than the Democrats to support. The conservative political action committees were alone in supporting challengers more than incumbents, but in their attempts to unseat liberal Democratic incumbents, these groups would find relatively fewer incumbents worthy of support. Whereas the 7 major liberal PACs spent 51 percent on House incumbents, the 15 major conservative PACs spent only 28 percent. Money, of course, is usually spent only when there is some expectation of success. Senate challengers received a larger proportion of funds than House challengers from all of these groups, but the Senate candidates were seen as more likely to win. Success, it appears, draws money, and money helps success.

Political action committees—in particular *conservative* political action committees—have been active in targeting Senate incumbents for defeat. In 1980, enormous amounts of money were spent by the National Conservative Political Action Committee (NCPAC) in helping conservative challengers defeat liberal Senate incumbents. Out of a total $3.15 million spent by the group, $1.2 million went to six Senate races. The money appeared well-spent; four of the liberal Democratic incumbents so targeted were defeated: George McGovern (S.D.), John Culver (Iowa), Frank Church (Idaho), and Birch Bayh (Ind.). The other two targeted senators—Democrats Alan Cranston of California and Thomas Eagleton of Missouri—won re-election. It remains unproven, of course, that conservative PAC money was responsible for the defeats. Republican party officials were quick to point out that the National Republican Senatorial Committee also worked hard and spent heavily on these races. Moreover, the four liberal Democrats were defeated in what could be considered traditionally Republican states. South Dakota, Idaho, Iowa, and Indiana—all had Republicans *already* elected for the other Senate seat. Clearly, the relationship between campaign spending, political action committees, and support for the challenger in defeating incumbents needs further investigation. But it is worth noting that liberal PACs have not yet mounted only major effort in response, nor has any PAC given more than a handful of House races a priority.

Broadcast Spending and Media Attention

Broadcast expenditures, especially for television, constitute the major item in many campaign budgets. Hence, questions about campaign spending lead easily to questions about broadcast spending and its effects. Unfortunately, very little attention has been paid to the subject in congressional campaigns. The few initial findings can be summarized briefly.

The candidate's share of broadcast expenditures is significantly related to the candidate's share of the vote, even when the effects of incumbency are controlled for.[25] Money spent on radio and television does affect the vote separately from whether one is helped or hurt by being, or opposing, an incumbent. Also, as might be expected, these effects are stronger in the Senate than in the House. House district lines, of course, do not follow television viewing boundaries. Candidates in some districts would be paying for a television audience extending to 10 or more districts while other candidates would find a much more economical voter audience. Nevertheless, even when this inequality is eliminated—by looking only at races where a candidate's boundaries would reach no more than two additional congressional districts—the effects of broadcast spending, while increased, are still relatively minor.[26]

Media spending, these studies argue, affects the vote by increasing the recognition of candidates, particularly those otherwise unknown. It provides that necessary minimal impact for voters to be aware that the candidate is in the contest and that a choice must be made. But does campaign broadcasting have any effects beyond this supplying of name recognition? One study that combines survey responses with campaign broadcasting information indicates yes. Beyond recognition, House broadcast spending shows a significant, although small, effect on the vote. "Voters," the study concludes, "are apparently gaining something from the media beyond mere familiarity with the candidate's name."[27] We can also look at the media contact that the voters perceive. One study examines the separate and interactive impact of a number of factors—including recognition, media contact, and other contact—on the voters' evaluations of the candidates. For both incumbents and challengers in the Senate and House, media contact retains an impact on candidate evaluations independent of the other effects.[28]

Media coverage, of course, extends beyond the efforts of the candidates themselves. News media report independently on the candidates and the campaign. One study of newspaper coverage of 1978 House races reveals several findings of interest.[29] Newspapers—primarily the largest circulation dailies in the area—were analyzed for their treatment of House races in districts where surveys were being conducted. As could be expected, the coverage of these contests appeared relatively low, averaging 11.9 articles and ads (0.8 front-page articles) with any mention of either candidate or the campaign generally. Races between incumbents and challengers, it is interesting to note, had slightly more coverage than open-seat races. The incumbent's name was mentioned more frequently than the challenger's and more frequently with a positive tone. The authors report that while there was little difference between the parties in the positive tone of the coverage, incumbents were much more likely than challengers to be described in positive terms.

Analysis showed that media coverage was indeed significantly related to the recognition of candidates and, as in the case of spending, more important for the challenger than for the incumbent. The tone of the coverage, however, did not appear to affect the evaluation of candidates. The usual speculation that a critical press affects the voters' views of the candidates was not supported by these results. Newspapers, however, can affect the vote through their impact on candidate recognition. Coverage affects recognition, particularly for the challenger, and recognition affects the vote.

More work will be needed to separate the effects of media spending from spending generally and from the media's coverage of the candidates and the campaign. At this point, however, it appears that all three factors are important in supplying information to voters—although more so for challengers than for incumbents.

These findings have relevance for the continuing debate about campaign spending reforms. With escalating campaign budgets running well beyond inflation, people worry about the big contributors and the fact that only personally wealthy candidates may be able to run for Congress, especially for the Senate where one must mount an expensive state-wide campaign. But campaign money may give challengers their only chance to offset the incumbents' many advantages. Spending buys challengers that necessary minimal visibility which incumbents already have at the start of a campaign. Therefore, reformers face an unpleasant choice of alternatives. Any reform that limits overall spending, limits broadcast spending, or otherwise curtails the congressional campaign, also hurts the challenger and further reduces the competitiveness of congressional races.

SUMMARY

We can look at these results in terms of the selection process outlined in Chapter 1. Information is low in congressional races compared to presidential contests, and it is lower in the House than in the Senate. Indeed, presidential voting provides a model for a high-information decision that few congressional races can emulate. These differences must be recognized before generalizing about "American voting behavior" or constructing models to explain that behavior. While some Senate races may approach the presidential information levels, with two highly visible candidates whose position and qualifications are thoroughly screened by the voters, most races are decided with much less information available. Still, Senate candidates are visible enough for their names to be recognized and to have had some contact with voters. The voters know a choice must be made and can use specific information for a decision. They have had "some contact with" or "learned something about" the two candidates. In many House races in contrast, no such choice may be recognized. Voters may decide that the candidate in office is good enough for them and not seek further information; or they may decide that the outcome is not worth the extensive digging for information about low-profile challengers; or both of these kinds of thinking may be at work simultaneously. Whatever the justification, for the majority of voters who know something about only one candidate, the choice is essentially over at stage one. They buy the product they have bought before.

People are many things besides citizens and must face, and manage to avoid, many decisions besides electoral ones. Candidates accordingly must cross a minimum threshold of voters' awareness; and the political context can help make this task easy or difficult. This chapter makes clear the importance of contextual influences. The office contested, the qualifications of candidates, and the amount of spending affect visibility and voting results. For some candidates, visibility is easily supplied by office support and past success. Others can purchase it, and still others, such as many House challengers, never achieve it at all. From this perspective we can understand the finding that money and media coverage help challengers much more than incumbents.

We should also be cautioned not to be too impressed with the office advantages of House incumbents. *Both* Senate and House incumbents enjoy the same office support, and yet one draws opponents who can get across to voters and the other does not. Both have staffs, free mailing, and publicity advantages from being in office. Both can advertise, claim credit for government help back home, and take positions that enhance their general reputation. And yet Senate incumbents are no longer perceived to be safe, while House incumbents remain so; and Senate incumbents attract active visible challenges and House incumbents do not. There appears, rather, to be a complex of reinforcing factors affecting the challenger's visibility and subsequent electoral success. An incumbent's perceived vulnerability, money, and media attention reinforce each other and help or hurt the candidate's task in getting some information across to voters.

Visibility is necessary, but not necessarily positive. How information is translated into voting decisions is the subject of the following chapters.

NOTES

1. Warren Miller and Donald Stokes, "Constituency Influence in Congress," *American Political Science Review* (March 1963): 45-57.
2. Barbara Hinckley, "Issues, Information Costs, and Congressional Elections," *American Politics Quarterly* (April 1976): 131-152. For similar results in the Senate, see Gary Jacobson, *Money in Congressional Elections* (New Haven: Yale University Press, 1980), p. 14.
3. Barbara Hinckley, Richard Hofstetter, and John Kessel, "Information and the Vote: A Comparative Election Study," *American Politics Quarterly* (April 1974): 131-158.
4. Based on results from the 1978 National Election Study, Center for Political Studies, University of Michigan.
5. Ibid.
6. For more details on the analysis, see Barbara Hinckley, "House Reelections and Senate Defeats: The Role of the Challenger," *British Journal of Political Science* (October 1980): 441-460. See also Alan Abramowitz, "A Comparison of Voting for U.S. Senator and Representative in 1978," *American Political Science Review* (September 1980): 633-640. Note that there are more Democratic party identifiers than Republicans in the sample, and in the nation, and that partisans are most apt to be familiar with their own party's candidates—hence the edge in recognition for Democratic over Republican candidates.
7. Warren Miller, "A Sourcebook of Selected Data," in *Sage Electoral Studies Yearbook*, vol. 6, ed. L. Sandy Maisel and Joseph Cooper (Beverly Hills: Sage Publications, 1981), tables 1-5, 2-2, and 2-9. No questions in the survey asked about attention to the House race specifically.
8. Thomas Mann, *Unsafe At Any Margin* (Washington, D.C.: American Enterprise Institute, 1978), p. 33. The polls were conducted by the Democratic Study Group for what were considered to be some key Democratic races.
9. Ibid., p. 40. The phrases were supplied by the interviewer.
10. Charles Jones, "The Role of the Campaign in Congressional Politics," in *The Electoral Process*, ed. Kent Jennings and Harmon Zeigler (Englewood Cliffs, N.J.: Prentice-Hall, 1966), p. 29.
11. Morris Fiorina, "The Case of the Vanishing Marginals: The Bureaucracy Did It," *American Political Science Review* (March 1977): 177-181.
12. David Mayhew, *Congress: The Electoral Connection* (New Haven: Yale University Press, 1974).
13. See Glenn Parker, "Sources of Change in Congressional District Attentiveness," *American Journal of Political Science* (February 1980): 115-124; and "Cycles in Congressional District Attention," *Journal of Politics* (May 1980): 540-548.
14. Richard Fenno, *Home Style* (Boston: Little, Brown & Co., 1978).
15. August 1980 mailing to constituents.
16. Jacobson, *Money in Congressional Elections*, pp. 228, 229.
17. The Federal Elections Campaign Act of 1971 required the first detailed reporting of campaign contributions and expenditures. The results are available for election years since 1972.
18. Jacobson, *Money in Congressional Elections*, pp. 228, 229.
19. Mark 4:25 (translation from *The Living Bible*).
20. Stanton Glantz et al., "Election Outcomes: Whose Money Matters," *Journal of Politics* (November 1976): 1033-1041; Gary Jacobson, "The Effects of

Campaign Spending on Congressional Elections," *American Political Science Review* (June 1978): 469-491; and Jacobson, *Money in Congressional Elections.*

21. Jacobson, *Money in Congressional Elections,* p. 42; see also Glantz et al., "Election Outcomes."
22. Jacobson, *Money in Congressional Elections,* pp. 136-162.
23. Ibid., p. 23.
24. For details, see Michael Malbin, "Of Mountains and Molehills: PACs, Campaigns, and Public Policy," in *Parties, Interest Groups, and Campaign Finance Laws,* ed. Michael Malbin (Washington, D.C.: American Enterprise Institute, 1980), pp. 160, 161. See also Jacobson, *Money in Congressional Elections,* pp. 88, 104.
25. Paul Dawson and James Zinser, "Broadcast Expenditures and Electoral Outcomes in the 1970 Congressional Elections," *Public Opinion Quarterly* (Fall 1971): 398-402; Gary Jacobson, "The Impact of Broadcast Campaigning on Electoral Outcomes," *Journal of Politics* (August 1975): 769-793; and Edie Goldenberg and Michael Traugott, "Campaign Effects on Outcomes in the 1978 Congressional Elections" (Paper presented at the Houston-Rice Conference on Congressional Elections, Houston, Texas, January 1980).
26. Jacobson, "The Impact of Broadcast Campaigning," pp. 782, 783.
27. Goldenberg and Traugott, "Campaign Effects on Outcomes," p. 19.
28. Lyn Ragsdale, "Incumbent Popularity, Challenger Invisibility, and Congressional Voters," *Legislative Studies Quarterly* (May 1981).
29. Edie Goldenberg and Michael Traugott, "Congressional Campaign Effects on Candidate Recognition and Evaluation," *Political Behavior* 1 (1980): 61-90.

3

The Effects of Incumbency

Voting is not idiosyncratic. Major influences can be identified that hold over time and across the great variety of congressional contests. Two such influences—incumbency and party—are examined in this and the following chapters. Together they can make sense of much of the congressional voting results.

THE ADVANTAGE OF INCUMBENCY

Members of Congress tend to return to Congress. In the study of congressional elections, the influence of incumbency is the first fact commanding attention. In the past, House and Senate incumbents of each party have enjoyed success rates of 80 to 90 percent; in other words, the incumbent who seeks re-election wins 80 to 90 times out of 100 races. Particularly in the House, the success rate is spectacular, holding consistently around 90 percent and reaching as high as 97 percent. One can compare these rates to those for incumbent governors (about 60 percent), some games of chance (50 percent), or other high-risk endeavors. In anyone's game, a 90 percent chance is a pretty good bet. In the 1980 election, which saw a dramatic sweep of presidential electoral votes and a change in party control of the White House and Senate, the House stayed remarkably the same. Of the 392 incumbents running in the general election, 92 percent were re-elected to the House.

Not only are House incumbents likely to win, but their winning margin is higher than that of victorious nonincumbents. One study determined that the value of running as a House incumbent, compared to running as a nonincumbent, accounted for about five percentage points in the results—the difference, for example, between someone gaining 60 or 55 percent of the vote in a district or someone gaining 54 compared to 49 percent.[1] Another study notes a "sophomore surge" or gain in the vote won between a member's first and second election to the House. Accompanying this surge is a "retirement slump" or loss in percent of the vote for the candidate of the same party as the retiring incumbent.[2]

Moreover, as we see from Table 3-1, neither primary defeats nor early retirements—from those who might see impending defeat—change the overall pattern. Incumbents are even safer at the primary stage than they are in the general election. Few need to contest primaries and, of those who do, most win. Nor do retirements, in the House at least, serve as a surrogate for election defeat. It is true that the number of members seeking re-election to both the House and Senate has declined slightly in recent years. But it would be difficult to argue, on looking closely at the results, that the decline significantly affects the overall safeness. In 1978, for example, of the 53 House members not seeking re-election, 4 died, 18 sought larger state-wide office (senator, governor, lieutenant governor or state attorney general), and 13 had reached or passed what is usually considered retirement age in American society. They were 65 or older. This leaves 18 members whose retirements are unexplained. Even if we assume quite unrealistically that all 18 retired to avoid election defeat (and so ignore ill health and other personal reasons), the incumbents' success rate remains impressive. If we add the 18 to those seeking re-election and assume all 18 were defeated, this means that 42 out of 400, or 9 percent, would lose, for a success rate of 90 percent.

The success of House incumbents is not new. A century-long trend marks the increasing stability of House membership and the corresponding decline in competition. Since the late 1800s, the proportion of House first-term members has declined, and the average number of terms served by members has increased. The number of seats changing from one party to the other has decreased correspondingly.[3] The House, originally designed to be the more popularly responsive chamber with elections every two years, has developed a membership stability to rival the Senate, where only one-third of the membership stands for re-election at any one time. When the 96th Congress convened following the 1978 elections, 20 of 100 senators, or 20 percent, were new to Congress. (Two-thirds of the members had not had to face re-election that year.) By comparison in the House, with all 435 seats contested, there were 88 new members, or 18 percent.

Although House safeness is not new, the trend appears to have accelerated in recent years. The same point can be seen by a number of measures: the incumbents' share of the vote is larger; the percentage point "value" of incumbency is greater; and the sophomore surge and retirement slump have increased.[4] While races between nonincumbents

Table 3-1 The Advantage of Incumbency in the House and Senate, 1946-1980

	House				Senate			
		Defeated				Defeated		
Year	Seeking Re-election	Primary	General	Percent Re-elected*	Seeking Re-election	Primary	General	Percent Re-elected*
1946	398	18	52	82.4	30	6	7	56.7
1948	400	15	68	79.2	25	2	8	60.0
1950	400	6	32	90.5	32	5	5	68.8
1952	389	9	26	91.0	31	2	9	64.5
1954	407	6	22	93.1	32	2	6	75.0
1956	411	6	16	94.6	29	0	4	86.2
1958	396	3	37	89.9	28	0	10	64.3
1960	405	5	25	92.6	29	0	1	96.6
1962	402	12	22	91.5	35	1	5	82.9
1964	397	8	45	86.6	33	1	4	84.8
1966	411	8	41	88.1	32	3	1	87.5
1968	409	4	9	96.8	28	4	4	71.4
1970	401	10	12	94.5	31	1	6	77.4
1972	390	12	13	93.6	27	2	5	74.1
1974	391	8	40	87.7	27	2	2	85.2
1976	384	3	13	95.8	25	0	9	64.0
1978	382	5	19	93.7	25	3	7	60.0
1980	398	6	31	90.7	29	4	9	55.2

* Counting both primary and general election defeats.

SOURCE: *Congressional Quarterly Weekly Report*, April 5, 1980, p. 908 and November 8, 1980, pp. 3302, 3320-3321.

remain competitive, competition in districts with incumbents has decreased. The "marginals," says David Mayhew, "are vanishing."[5]

Nevertheless, this emphasis on House safeness requires three points of qualification. First, membership turnover does occur. Even if only 18 percent of the House and Senate are new after each election, in six years more than half of the Congress would be changed. In actual fact, a majority of the 96th Congress elected in 1978 had not been present for the Nixon impeachment debate and resignation or for the passage of the War Powers Act in 1973. About one-third (35 percent) could remember the Vietnam debates in Congress in 1969 and 1970.

Second, care is needed in distinguishing precisely what phenomenon we are trying to explain. Many people speak of "the decline of competition in congressional elections," but the phrase needs clarification. How is "competition" to be measured, and what is meant by "congressional"? As Table 3-2 indicates, the proportion of safe seats in the House has increased since 1956—if one looks at the proportion of seats that incumbents have won by 60 percent or more of the vote. But if one looks instead at the proportion of seats lost by incumbents, no similar trend is apparent: *the proportion remains small throughout the time period.* And if one looks at the Senate, the proportion of safe seats has not increased,[6] and the proportion of incumbents losing re-election appears, if anything, to be rising. In other words, Table 3-2 supplies four different measures of competition in congressional elections: according to one measure, it is declining; according to another, it is increasing; and according to the other two, it is remaining about the same.

Third and most critically, writers concerned with the House have missed what may be an important developing Senate trend. While the Senate re-election rates show considerable fluctuation, they have dropped noticeably in the past several years. Fewer senators run for re-election, and fewer win. A comparison of 1976, 1978, and 1980 general election results is instructive. In 1976, House incumbents won 97 percent of their bids for re-election; Senate incumbents 64 percent. In 1978, House incumbents won 95 percent; Senate incumbents 68 percent. And in 1980, House incumbents won 92 percent, and Senate incumbents won 64 percent. In the Senate, it would appear, it is not the marginals, but the incumbents, who are vanishing. Clearly, any explanations of why incumbents are so advantaged must consider the Senate as well as the House results.

SOURCES OF SUPPORT

What is it that voters know and like about incumbents that can help explain their electoral advantage? And what is it about House incumbents, compared to other candidates, that explains their particu-

Table 3-2   Safe Seats in the House and Senate, 1956-1978

	House Incumbents					Senate Incumbents			
	Winning by 60+% of the Vote[1]		Losing the Election[2]			Winning by 60+% of the Vote[1]		Losing the Election[2]	
	N	%	N	%		N	%	N	%
1956	(403)	59	(405)	4	1956-60	(84)	43	(86)	17
1958	(390)	63	(393)	9					
1960	(400)	59	(400)	6					
1962	(376)	64	(390)	6	1962-66	(86)	44	(96)	10
1964	(388)	59	(389)	12					
1966	(401)	68	(403)	10					
1968	(397)	72	(405)	2	1968-72	(74)	45	(79)	19
1970	(389)	77	(391)	3					
1972	(373)	78	(378)	3					
1974	(383)	66	(383)	10	1974-78	(70)	41	(75)	24
1976	(381)	72	(381)	3					
1978	(377)	78	(377)	5					
1980	(392)	(72)	(392)	(8)					

[1] Cover-Mayhew measure, as reported in "Congressional Dynamics and the Decline of Competitive Congressional Elections," in *Congress Reconsidered*, 2nd ed., edited by Lawrence C. Dodd and Bruce I. Oppenheimer (Washington, D.C.: Congressional Quarterly, 1981), p. 63. Cover and Mayhew define incumbents as those who have won a previous election and not as those in office at the time of election; hence the numbers in the columns of the table will not be identical. The 1980 calculations are based on the unofficial election returns recorded in *Congressional Quarterly Weekly Report*, November 8, 1980, pp. 3338-3345.

[2] Based on data included in Table 3-1 from *Congressional Quarterly Weekly Report*, April 5, 1980, p. 908, and November 8, 1980, pp. 3302, 3320-3321.

lar success? Survey responses supply some first answers to these two questions.

A picture emerges quite clearly of a pervasive general support. Representatives are liked, considered generally helpful, rated well on job performance, and, when issues can be identified by respondents, seen as agreeing generally with the respondent's views on issues. Representatives receive the warmest ratings on the feeling thermometers of any candidates and mostly get "good" or "very good" job ratings. Table 3-3 shows the extent—and the similarity—of this general support on a number of measures. Large majorities give positive responses, very few people give negative responses, and most people can answer the questions.[7]

It is more difficult, however, to pin down the specific components of this general support. When asked specific questions about what their representative had done to merit these positive impressions, many respondents—and voters—gave "Don't Know" responses. While 78 percent of the voters thought their representative would be helpful in dealing with a constituent's problem, only 22 percent had ever asked for such help, and only 28 percent knew of someone else who had. (Many of these are the same people.) People were asked, "Do you happen to remember anything special that your U.S. Representative [name supplied] has done for this district or for the people in this district while [he or she] has been in Congress?" This open-ended question searches for "anything" the respondent might have in mind that helps contribute to the generally favorable response. However, 80 percent of the national sample, and 69 percent of the voters, could not think of anything to answer the question—for representatives working so hard at constituency service and credit claiming activities, hardly a gratifying response!

In the list below, note the diminishing number of cases as one moves from general to specific questions of support. Of the 2304 respondents in the sample,

1760 said they had some contact with their representative;

1406 felt their representative could be at least somewhat helpful if they had a problem the representative could do something about;

1058 gave representatives "good" or "very good" job ratings;

650 said they agreed at least somewhat with their representative's voting in Congress (a large majority, 1335, could not answer the question);

458 said they could remember something the representative had done while in Congress for the district or its people;

293 preferred one of the candidates because of an issue in the campaign, and of these, 184 preferred an incumbent (664 could identify such an issue of at least some importance to them);

Table 3-3   Support for House Incumbents (N=757)

| | Percentage of Voters | | | |
	Job Rating	Helpfulness	Feeling Thermometer	Vote
High Support	Very Good 20	Very 36	Very Warm 38	For 79
	Good 44	Somewhat 42	Warm 35	
	Fair 22	It Depends 3	Neutral 18	
Low Support	Poor 4	Not Very 7	Cold 8	Against 21
	Don't Know 10	Don't Know 12		
Total	(100%)	(100%)	(99%)	(100%)

NOTE: Compiled by the author from data from the 1978 National Election Study. The *job rating* question asked, "In general, how would you rate the job that your U.S. Representative [name supplied] has been doing — very good, good, fair, poor, or very poor?" The *helpfulness* question asked, "If you had a problem that Representative [name supplied] could do something about, do you think [he or she] would be very helpful, somewhat helpful, or not very helpful to you?" The *feeling thermometer* asked people to rate how they felt about the candidates on a scale from 100 degrees (most positive) to zero degrees (most negative). In the table, ratings from 80 degrees and warmer are labeled very warm, from 60 to 79 warm, from 50 to 59 and don't knows as neutral, and anything lower than 50 degrees as cold.

221 could remember a particular bill the representative voted on, and 151 agreed with the representative's vote.

The small number of responses to specific questions should be kept in mind in any attempt to explain the incumbent's popularity. It is true that the specific positive responses can be correlated with the general positive responses and with the vote: in other words, those who could think of something special their representatives had done would be even more likely than the others to rate them highly and vote for them and less likely to vote against them. It is also true that small numbers of people can make a difference in an election result. But people who could not think of anything special *also* rate representatives highly and vote for them. The number of specific responses is too small in itself to bear any major burden of explanation.

There is, nonetheless, some specific content beyond the generally favorable impressions. In response to open-ended questions, respondents can give reasons for liking and disliking candidates. While the reasons supplied tend to be fairly general themselves, they can be distinguished by subject matter, such as by references to issues, candidate qualifications, or other topics.[8]

These likes and dislikes, asked for House races in 1978, are shown in Table 3-4 for incumbents and their opponent-challengers.[9] People could give more than one positive or negative response; they could also say that there was nothing they liked or disliked about the House candidates. Thus the numbers reported in the table represent the separate comments that were made. As we might expect, (1) the number of likes for incumbents far outnumbers the number of dislikes; and (2) the number of comments for incumbents, whether positive or negative, far outnumbers the comments for opponent-challengers. What comments there are for challengers are more evenly divided between likes and dislikes. People have a lot to say about liking incumbents, not too much to say about disliking them, and not much to say about the challengers at all.

Table 3-4 reveals three findings of particular interest. First, of all the reasons for liking or disliking House candidates, personal qualities are the most frequently cited. These, plus the office-related qualities of experience and ability, dominate the table. In these races it is the perception of candidates—not of parties or issues—that emerges as important from the open-ended questions. House incumbents are liked for these candidate qualifications, as well as disliked, and they are also liked for their district attention. Something they do for the district—or are expected to do—is seen as a reason for liking them. District attention is cited frequently only for liking incumbents; it is not cited as a comment relevant to disliking them or to liking or disliking challengers.

Table 3-4   Likes and Dislikes about Incumbents and Their Challengers (Percentage of Responses)

	Democratic Incumbent		Republican Challenger	
	Likes $N=693$	Dislikes $N=169$	Likes $N=86$	Dislikes $N=79$
Experience/Ability	22	17	13	6
District Attention	30	8	2	0
Personal Qualities	26	46	49	41
Party	3	8	7	37
Ideology/Issues	9	14	22	11
Group Identification	5	6	4	1
Miscellaneous	6	2	4	4
Total Responses	(100%)	(101%)	(101%)	(99%)

	Republican Incumbent		Democratic Challenger	
	Likes $N=524$	Dislikes $N=104$	Likes $N=99$	Dislikes $N=70$
Experience/Ability	25	15	14	23
District Attention	19	11	6	3
Personal Qualities	28	30	53	27
Party	3	14	9	24
Ideology/Issues	15	17	21	13
Group Identification	5	8	3	1
Miscellaneous	4	5	4	9
Total Responses	(100%)	(100%)	(99%)	(100%)

SOURCE: Adapted from Glenn Parker, "Incumbent Popularity and Electoral Success," *Sage Electoral Studies Yearbook*, vol. 6, ed. L. Sandy Maisel and Joseph Cooper (Beverly Hills: Sage Publications, 1981), table 4.

NOTE: Based on all respondents in incumbent-contested races where the two major parties had candidates contesting. Respondents could give one, more than one, or no response to each of the like and dislike questions. Percentages may not sum to 100 because of rounding.

The respondents, therefore, appear to be understanding the activity and using it appropriately in their open-ended remarks.

Second, district attention appears more important for Democrats than for Republicans. The Democrats, of course, have long been the party in control of Congress and the one most closely associated with public works and other federal projects. District attention, then, might be particularly a Democratic party phenomenon and a help to keeping Democratic incumbents in Congress.

Third, the contrast between incumbents and challengers should be noted. Issues and parties, cited relatively infrequently for incumbents, appear more important in the comments for challengers. Ideology and issues become reasons for liking challengers while party is a reason for disliking them. Of course, with the low information about challengers generally, their political party may be the only thing known and the only way to express a negative response. Both Republicans and Democrats elicit negative reactions because of their party affiliations.

It is clear from Table 3-4 that respondents can give reasons for liking incumbents. These reasons center on candidate qualifications—both personal qualities and experience and ability—and their attentiveness to the district. We do not know, however, nor could we discover from surveys, whether the specific reason for liking contributes to the general support or is merely a rationalization from it. People may observe the incumbent's experience in office and conclude that this is a good thing and a reason for support, *or* people who support the incumbent and who are required to give reasons for doing so might say well, of course, the incumbent is more experienced. What we can conclude is that the very things emphasized by incumbents in their dealings with constituents are also emphasized by constituents in their open-ended remarks. This fact is important and deserves elaboration.

Richard Fenno has studied how representatives act in their districts when they make their visits home.[10] Members present themselves to constituents as individuals and as people who can be trusted. Members believe constituents want to judge them as people, as human beings. They want to "size you up" and "get the feel of you," in the members' own language, "as a person," and "as a human being." Members also seek to win the trust of constituents, but trust can be an elusive thing—won more by a pattern and style of behavior and a general impression than by any particular words or actions. Trust, according to Fenno, takes time and a continuing presence in the district. It is typically conveyed by giving constituents a sense of the incumbent's qualifications for the job; a sense of identification—that the representative is part of the district and one of its people; and a sense of empathy—that the representative cares about the people and understands them.

From this standpoint, district visits may be less important for what they do concretely than for what they communicate generally about the representative's concern and continued availability. Issues become less important in themselves than for the style they convey. They become vehicles, when used at all, primarily for the presentation of self. Also we can see the difficulties challengers must confront. Both qualifications and time spent for trust are incumbent commodities.

The emphasis, therefore, is on the personal and the general in conveying an elusive, but powerful "trusted" impression. The same impression is substantiated by the survey results, where once again we find emphasis on the personal and the general. People who like incumbents for their "experience," "competence," "honesty," or "integrity" and who have little more specific content to add may be receiving precisely the impression that was conveyed. (The first two comments presumably would be coded in the category of Experience/Ability and the second two under Personal Qualities.) The same would hold for those who believe their representatives care about the district but who cannot remember anything special that these representatives ever did. By this interpretation, it was the sense of caring that was communicated and received. In short, the survey results may be reflecting quite accurately what incumbents convey and what constituents receive.

House-Senate Differences

A major question, however, remains to be answered. What is it about House incumbents, compared to other candidates, that can explain their particular success? Senate incumbents enjoy the same institutional support and visibility as their House counterparts. They, too, as we will see, are evaluated positively. But they do not enjoy the same election results. In 1978, representatives won 94 percent of their bids for re-election and senators 60 percent. While 79 percent of voters in the survey reported voting for House incumbents, 61 percent reported voting for Senate incumbents. Senators, quite understandably, might not be too impressed with the advantages of congressional incumbency. Any explanations for House incumbents must deal with these differences in Senate and House results.

If we compare incumbents in the two chambers, few differences appear.[11] Both senators and representatives are in contact with the voters and are recognized by them, as we saw in Chapter 2. It is true that House incumbents show higher levels of personal contact than the senators; more people had met their representatives personally (23 percent of the voters) or had attended meetings where they spoke (21 percent). But Table 3-5 makes clear that meeting or not meeting House incumbents makes no significant difference to the vote. Nor is much difference found for attending meetings: all one could say is that the 28 people of the challenger's party who attended meetings with incumbents were indeed more likely to vote for the incumbent than the 155 people who did not![12] In short, there is little support overall for the argument that representatives' personal contact explains part of their voting advantage.

Another possible explanation of the incumbents' advantage in the House can also be eliminated. It might be asked whether different

expectations about the job of senator or representative underlie the
different results. Voters' expectations for the House might be more
easily satisfied than those for the Senate, reducing the need to seek
alternative candidates. The survey asked people to rank the following
list of congressional activities for both the Senate and House in order
from most to least important:

(1) Helping people in the district who have personal problems with
government;

(2) Making sure the district gets its fair share of government money
and projects;

(3) Keeping track of the way government agencies are carrying out laws
passed by Congress;

(4) Keeping in touch with the people about what the government is
doing;

(5) Working in Congress on bills concerning national issues.

If expectations for the House center on the district-related and the
personal (categories 1, 2, and 4) and those for the Senate on the national
and controversial (category 5 and possibly 3), this might help explain
the difference in success.

Such a possibility, however, is not supported by the results. While
voters vary a great deal in their expectations, they rate as most
important for both the Senate and the House categories 4 and 5: keeping
in touch with the people and legislating in Congress. As the most
important House activity, voters most frequently cite keeping in touch
(category 4) and next most frequently cite legislating in Congress

Table 3-5   House Incumbents' Personal Contact and the Vote

		Percentage Voting for Incumbent				
Personal Contact	N	Voters of Incumbent's Party	N	Inde-pendents	N	Voters of Challenger's Party
Met Personally						
Yes	(81)	96	(62)	87	(33)	52
No	(237)	96	(193)	78	(150)	45
Attended Meeting						
Yes	(71)	97	(56)	86	(28)	64
No	(247)	96	(199)	79	(155)	43 *

*An asterisk indicates a tau b for the relationship significant at the .05 level. Five of the six
crosstabulations reported in the table are not significant at this level.
SOURCE: Calculated by the author from data in the 1978 National Election Study.

Table 3-6   House and Senate Job Expectations and the Vote

	House			Senate		
	N	Percent Rating Most Important	Percent Voting for In- cumbent	N	Percent Rating Most Important	Percent Voting for In- cumbent
Helping people in the district	(73)	10	82	(42)	11	62
Making sure the district gets its fair share	(105)	14	70	(61)	15	62
Keeping track of government agencies	(131)	17	79	(63)	16	49
Keeping in touch with the people	(207)	27	81	(84)	21	62
Working in Con- gress on bills	(189)	25	78	(116)	29	62
All or None Important; Don't Know	(52)	7	83	(29)	7	69
Total	(757)	100%		(395)	99%	

NOTE: The question supplied the list of congressional activities and asked respondents to rank them in order of importance: the "most important activity" representatives or senators should be pursuing on down to the "least important activity." The table reports results for the most important activity cited.

(category 5). For the Senate, the order of preference is reversed. Combining first and second preferences, in both the Senate and House, voters most frequently cite keeping in touch. The least important activity in both chambers (with the least frequent first mentions and the most frequent least-important mentions) is category 1: helping individuals with government problems. Moreover, the choice of most important activity by and large makes no difference to the vote.

Table 3-6 shows the vote in terms of the most important activity cited. House voters support incumbents at essentially the same rate (within five percentage points), no matter which most important activity is cited. The one exception is the category 2 voters who emphasize the district's "fair share." Among Senate voters, the percentages are identical for four of the categories, with the only exception category 3 voters, those emphasizing oversight of government agencies. Whether people cite one category or another or all or none as most important, they are about equally likely to vote for the incumbent—at very high rates in the House and lower rates in the Senate. We do not know at this point whether the exceptions are merely products of certain 1978 campaigns or would be found to hold upon further examination. Nevertheless, the results are primarily important in eliminating differences in job expectations as explanations of the difference in the House and Senate vote.

Overall, the few differences observable between Senate and House incumbents make no difference to the results. It is with the challengers, rather, where the critical differences appear. As we saw in the preceding chapter, House challengers stand apart from all other candidates in their low visibility and contact with voters. Whereas Senate incumbents faced challengers recognized by 85 percent of the voters, House incumbents faced challengers recognized by 44 percent. Senate races, then, provide a choice between two candidates known and in contact with voters while many House races do not.

This point has further and very sizable implications. Table 3-7 shows the voters' evaluation of Senate and House candidates based on the feeling thermometers, scoring the inability to recognize and rate the candidates as a neutral 50 degrees.[13] Note, first, that *the Senate evaluations are primarily positive and similar to the ratings for House incumbents.* Working in the Senate does not bring substantial voter dissatisfaction. While House incumbents receive somewhat higher ratings, the incumbents in both chambers appear to be supported by the voters.

Note, second, the difference in the evaluation for challengers. *Senate challengers are more competitive with their opponents than House challengers,* as measured by the thermometer ratings. House incumbents edge Senate incumbents, who in turn edge Senate challengers—all scoring positive average ratings—and House challengers bring up the rear. Only 27 percent of the House voters gave challengers anything other than a neutral 50 degree rating. Even those voters who can recognize and rate the House challenger (shown in the final column in the table) give predominantly neutral scores.

Finally, it is important to see that *there is little negative perception of any congressional candidates,* whether Senate or House, incumbents or challengers. In House races, only 8 and 10 percent respectively give incumbents and challengers ratings of less than 50 degrees, while in Senate races 20 and 21 percent respectively give these ratings.

Congressional elections are less a matter of tossing the rascals out or screening would-be rascals from getting in than of getting beyond a neutral rating. For a large number of House voters, essentially no choice is provided: one candidate is known and the opponent is not. In many other contests in both the Senate and House, the choice involves either two positive or one positive and one neutral perception. House challengers, even when recognized, retain primarily neutral ratings. But given the overall positive evaluation of congressional candidates, it is the neutral score that loses the election.

It appears from this first analysis that at least two separate factors are at work. House incumbents enjoy a strong, if general, margin of support, but they *also* enjoy—in contrast to senators—the boon of fairly invisible challengers. Each component, of course, can contribute to and interact with the other. Popular incumbents can discourage strong challengers from entering the race. Serious challengers can reduce the

Table 3-7   Feeling Thermometer Ratings by Type of Candidate

Degrees on Thermometer	Percentage of Voters Rating				
	House Incumbents	Senate Incumbents	Senate Challengers	House Challengers	House Challengers II
100	15	10	5	1	2
90-99	1	0	0	0	1
80-89	22	19	12	3	7
70-79	19	17	15	5	12
60-69	16	15	15	8	17
50-59	18	20	33	74	41
40-49	3	7	9	4	8
30-39	2	4	4	2	4
20-29	0	0	0	0	0
10-19	1	4	4	2	3
0-9	2	5	4	2	4
Total	(99%)	(101%)	(101%)	(101%)	(99%)
Number of Cases	757	395	395	757	334
Mean Degrees	68.9	61.3	56.5	51.3	52.9
Standard Deviation	21.7	25.1	21.6	12.6	18.8

NOTE: The first four columns are based on all voters in contested two-party elections with incumbents. Those who cannot recognize and rate the candidates are scored as 50 degrees. The final column of the table, labelled House Challengers II, shows the distribution for those who can recognize and rate the challengers. Percentages may not sum to 100 because of rounding.

incumbent's popularity during the campaign as weak points are targeted and alternatives made known. House incumbents' ratings, therefore, might be reduced and brought even closer to the Senate ratings merely by increasing the competition.[14]

Explaining the Vote

The results from this and the preceding chapter can be used to explain the vote: i.e., whether people vote for the incumbent or challenger in Senate and House races. Taking the vote as the outcome to be explained—or dependent variable—we can measure the effects of the following four influences, or independent variables:

- party identification
- recognition of the challenger
- relative contact by the two candidates
- relative evaluation of the two candidates.

The voter's party identification, as will be seen in Chapter 4, affects the vote independently of the incumbency-related influences. The relative evaluation of candidates—as measured by "liking" on the feeling thermometer—should also affect the vote independently of the candidate's visibility; and visibility should be important independently of the relative evaluations. House incumbents are advantaged both by being liked for what they do and by having invisible challengers. Since information varies so much in congressional races, visibility is best measured at two levels: at a minimum threshold of whether a candidate is recognized as being in the race; and, once that threshold is passed, at the level of relative visibility for the two candidates.

These four possible influences can be measured as follows from what voters report in their survey responses: party identification (the same as the incumbent, no identification, or the same as the challenger); challenger recognition (whether one can or cannot even recognize the challenger's name); relative contact by the candidates (the number of different kinds of contact cited for the incumbent minus the number cited for the challenger); and relative evaluations (the incumbent's degree rating on the thermometer minus the challenger's degree rating, scoring the inability to rate as 50 degrees). We can then examine statistically the independent influence of each of these components separately from the effects of the others.

The results for both the Senate and the House are similar and clear. Each component contributes an independent and significant influence on the vote. Party identification, challenger recognition, relative contact, and relative evaluations—all are important independently of each other.[15] The advantage of "incumbency" in congressional elections, then, can be seen as operating both through visibility and relative evaluations. The results hold for both the Senate and House, but in the Senate, we know, challengers are competitive in both visibility and evaluations. In the House, each of these influences that affects the vote favors one candidate over the other.

THE LIMITS OF INCUMBENCY

Even in the House, incumbents can be defeated—or made to run a very close race. As a preliminary analysis subject to future testing, three major patterns can be proposed. While these are the exceptions in view of the overall success rate, they add an important perspective to the more general rule.

Negative Voting

First, it appears that incumbents can be defeated through negative voting. People vote against some perception related to the incumbents themselves or their behavior in office. Scandals, for example, offer particularly clear occasions to see the effects of negative voting. In 1978, of three members reprimanded by the House for accepting favors from South Korean lobbyist Tongsun Park, two were re-elected, and one was defeated. Of two others indicted for bribery and conflict of interest, one was elected, and one was defeated. Scandals are not enough necessarily to override the incumbent's advantage, but they do lower the success rate. Altogether, three of these five, or 60 percent, were re-elected. In 1980, five Democrats faced scandals from the Abscam investigation in which the FBI had purported to offer certain representatives bribes in return for legislative favors. Four of the five were defeated. Two other representatives were also involved in scandals: one, a Republican, charged with soliciting sex from a 16-year-old boy; and the other, a Democrat, charged with deliberate misuse of office funds. The first was defeated and the second re-elected.

In a more systematic study of these effects, John Peters and Susan Welch examine the electoral impact of charges of corruption for House races from 1968 through 1978.[16] Of a total of 80 representatives facing corruption charges during this period, 65 ran for re-election, and 49 won. The success rate for those running was 75 percent re-elected, and the total return rate—i.e., those returning to the House for the next Congress—was 61 percent. In other words, incumbents facing charges of corruption are less likely to win re-election than other House incumbents (with a success rate of 75 percent compared to a success rate of more than 90 percent), and less likely to return to Congress. Still, three-fourths do win re-election, and about 60 percent return.

Peters and Welch also examine the effects of corruption on the vote margin: while safe representatives may survive, they may suffer a loss in their percentage of the vote. The authors calculate an expected vote, based on past electoral performance, and compare the actual vote received with that expectation. They find that incumbents charged with corruption lose, on the average, from 6 to 11 percentage points from the expected vote margin. Republicans lose on the average 6 percentage points and Democrats 11 percentage points. The type of corruption charge appears to affect the amount of electoral retribution. Morals charges bring the greatest vote losses—from 15 percentage points in vote margin for Republicans to 22 percentage points for Democrats. Bribery charges account for the next greatest vote losses—from 13 percentage points for Republicans to 18 percentage points for Democrats. Conflict of interest charges do not bring a significant vote loss, nor do other kinds of corruption charges. Overall, however, it appears that negative voting can defeat or seriously challenge incumbents, with charges about morals and bribery offering the clearest illustrations of this effect.

Perceptions of Vulnerability

Second, incumbents can be defeated through the circular effects of vulnerability. Representatives perceived to be vulnerable from past election results attract stronger challenges for future elections. At least we know that *the incumbents defeated in any one election will show disproportionately clear tendencies of being vulnerable in the preceding election.* Of the 19 House incumbents defeated in 1978, a total of 12—or 63 percent—had won re-election in 1976 by less than 55 percent of the vote. In contrast, only 76 of all of the 435 representatives winning in 1976—or 17 percent—had won by less than 55 percent of the vote. If one adds those incumbents facing scandals in 1978 to those seen as electorally vulnerable from the 1976 results, 14 of the 19 House incumbents defeated in 1978 could be termed vulnerable before the election. One additional defeated incumbent had won in a special election by 55 percent of the vote and never faced a general election contest. He, too, would be considered vulnerable in 1978.

We know also that *the incumbents who are defeated will have faced challengers very atypical in terms of their campaign spending.* Whereas most challengers spend far less than the incumbents they are running against, more than half of the victorious challengers in 1978 spent more than their respective incumbents. (See Appendix Table A-5 on page 150.) Finally, we know that *the challenger's spending in any one election year appears to follow the incumbent's vulnerability in the past election year.* As Table 3-8 makes clear, very few challengers spend more than incumbents who have won their preceding election by a sizable

Table 3-8   Incumbent Marginality and Challenger Spending in the House, 1978

Incumbent's Victory Margin in 1976		Challenger Outspent Incumbent in 1978	
Percentage of Total Vote	N	N	Percentage of Cases
Under 55.0	62	23	37
55.0-55.9	60	7	12
60.0 or more	255	28	11

SOURCE: Spending reports are taken from Michael Barone et al., *The Almanac of American Politics, 1980* (New York: E. P. Dutton, 1979); 1976 election results are taken from Congressional Quarterly, *Electing Congress* (Washington, D.C.: Congressional Quarterly, 1978) and 1978 election results from *Congressional Quarterly Weekly Report*, November 11, 1978, pp. 3283-3290. Races won by 60% or more of the vote include uncontested races.

margin: i.e., 55 percent or more of the vote. In contrast, more than one-third of the challengers spend more than incumbents who won their preceding election narrowly.

Of course, it is extremely difficult to separate, within such a circularly reinforcing process, the causes of vulnerability from the effects. Nevertheless, the surface evidence suggests that the perception of past vulnerability can contribute to an incumbent's election defeat. If this is indeed the case, members of Congress may need to do more than work to win re-election: they may need to win so substantially in any one year that they discourage opposition for the next time around.

The "Challenger Blitz"

Third, incumbents can be defeated through exceptional activity by the challenger—a kind of challenger blitz. The incumbents may have done nothing wrong. They may have maintained their district attention and done all the constituency service and other good things described throughout the chapter. Nevertheless, sufficient funding and activity on the part of the challenger can produce a close race, to be decided either way depending on the partisanship of the district, the issues, and other events of the time. It is worth noting that of the four defeated 1978 incumbents who were not vulnerable from scandals or previous election results, three faced challenges showing exceptionally large increases in spending compared to the past. In 1980, a number of House Democrats faced opponents strongly supported by national organized party and nonparty groups. While most won re-election—although more narrowly than in the past—a few were defeated.

These losses, however, are the exception. The news accounts herald all the incumbents who lose, with no mention made of the 350 or so who win. In 1978, while 19 incumbents were defeated, 358 won—255 by at least 60 percent of the vote. In 1980, while 31 incumbents were losing, 360 won—284 by at least 60 percent.[17] Nevertheless, these House exceptions—of negative voting, perceived vulnerability, and exceptionally strong and well-funded challengers—are becoming more common in Senate races. It is possible, then, that the Senate provides a glimpse of the future of House results.

SUMMARY

The advantages and limits of incumbency can make sense in terms of the discussion in the previous two chapters. In House races, two things appear to be working simultaneously. Representatives spend time and effort building trust and a generally positive impression, but they do this in a context where the alternatives are not known. In a majority of House races, voters cannot recognize the challengers, rate how they feel about them, or make any comments about why they like or dislike them. From the standpoint of the voters, this need not be an ill-considered selection. The incumbent, remember, is doing a "good job," and so there is no need to extend the process of decision. The same two components—incumbent's support and challenger's visibility—can explain the very different Senate results. Senators, too, are generally liked and positively rated. They may work just as hard as representatives in building trust and support, although we cannot know this until we ask comparable House and Senate questions. But we do know that, in contrast to representatives, senators work in a context of information where their opponent-challengers are known. Alternatives are posed for the decision.

Of course some House voters, too, will be considering the opposing candidates: for instance, some portion of that minority of voters who can say something at all about the challengers. Clearly, also, incumbency gives no blank checks for representatives. If negative information gets across to voters—a scandal, an issue hurting the incumbent, a mood against incumbents generally—then we would expect the decision process to be extended to a search for alternatives. Scandals do not necessarily override incumbency, but they do lower the success rate. Similarly, if enough positive information gets across to voters—through the activity and funding of a challenger's campaign—voters also must choose between two alternatives.

The Senate-House differences raise some additional and serious questions. We saw earlier that information varies with a number of factors including the challenger's spending. We now see that the visibility of the challenger is directly related to the vote. While the question needs much more attention, part of the recent upsurge in Senate competition may be a product of increased challenger spending.

If this is the case, any move to increase House competition and save the endangered "vanishing marginals" has to face the issues of campaign spending and who the campaign contributors will be.

Incumbency may be the first factor to recognize in congressional voting, but it is not the only one. Other influences on the vote—party identification, the candidates, and the issues—will be addressed in the following chapters.

NOTES

Portions of this chapter draw on an earlier article by the author entitled "House Reelections and Senate Defeats," *British Journal of Political Science* (October 1980): 441-460.

1. Robert Erikson, "Malapportionment, Gerrymandering, and Party Fortunes in Congressional Elections," *American Political Science Review* (December 1972): 1240. The question of incumbency has received major attention in past congressional elections research. See, for example, Robert Erikson, "The Advantage of Incumbency in Congressional Elections," *Polity* (Spring 1971): 395-405; Charles Jones, *Every Second Year* (Washington, D.C.: The Brookings Institution, 1967); Barbara Hinckley, "Incumbency and the Presidential Vote in Senate Elections," *American Political Science Review* (September 1970): 836-842; Warren Kostroski, "Party and Incumbency in Postwar Senate Elections," *American Political Science Review* (December 1973): 1213-1234; Albert Cover, "One Good Term Deserves Another," *American Journal of Political Science* (August 1977): 523-542; and Candice Nelson, "The Effect of Incumbency on Voting in Congressional Elections, 1964-1974," *Political Science Quarterly* (Winter 1978/1979): 665-678. The most recent studies of incumbency are cited in footnote 7.
2. Albert Cover and David Mayhew, "Congressional Dynamics and the Decline of Competitive Congressional Elections," in *Congress Reconsidered,* 2nd ed., edited by Lawrence C. Dodd and Bruce I. Oppenheimer (Washington, D.C.: Congressional Quarterly, 1981), pp. 62-82.
3. Nelson Polsby, "The Institutionalization of the U.S. House of Representatives," *American Political Science Review* 62 (1968): 144-168; Morris Fiorina et al., "Historical Change in House Turnover," in *Congress in Change,* ed. Norman Ornstein (New York: Praeger Publishers, 1975); Charles Bullock III, "House Careerists: Changing Patterns of Longevity and Attrition," *American Political Science Review* 66 (1972): 1295-1305.
4. See Cover and Mayhew, "Congressional Dynamics."
5. David Mayhew, "Congressional Elections: The Case of the Vanishing Marginals," *Polity* (Spring 1974): 295-317. A "marginal" district is a competitive district, traditionally defined either as won by less than 55 percent of the vote or less than 60 percent.
6. Cover and Mayhew, "Congressional Dynamics," p. 64. The authors divide the Senate, but not the House, into northern and southern seats won by at least 60 percent of the major party vote. In the same time period shown for the House, southern safe seats have declined, while northern safe seats, after rising in the early 1960s, have remained stable. The breakdown is as follows:

	Percentage	
	South	North
1956-60	96	24
1962-66	70	36
1968-72	71	38
1974-78	57	38

7. The data are from the 1978 National Election Study, Center for Political Studies, University of Michigan. Each of the measures is quite strongly correlated with each other and with the vote, with correlations (Pearson's r) in the range of .5 and .6. For studies using these data to analyze incumbency, see Alan Abramowitz, "A Comparison of Voting for U.S. Senator and Representative in 1978," *American Political Science Review* (September 1980): 633-640; Thomas Mann and Raymond Wolfinger, "Candidates and Parties in Congressional Elections," *American Political Science Review* (September 1980): 617-632; Barbara Hinckley, "House Reelections and Senate Defeats: The Role of the Challenger," *British Journal of Political Science* (October 1980): 441-460; Gary Jacobson, "Congressional Elections, 1978: The Case of the Vanishing Challengers," *Sage Electoral Studies Yearbook*, vol. 6, ed. L. Sandy Maisel and Joseph Cooper (Beverly Hills: Sage Publications, 1981).

8. For the use of these open-ended questions in presidential elections, see Angus Campbell et al., *The American Voter* (New York: John Wiley & Sons, 1960), chap. 3; in Senate elections, see Gerald Wright, *Electoral Choice in America* (Chapel Hill: Institute for Research in Social Science, 1974) and Barbara Hinckley et al., "Information and the Vote: A Comparative Election Study," *American Politics Quarterly* (April 1974): 131-158; and for past House elections, see Alan Abramowitz, "Name Familiarity, Reputation, and the Incumbency Effect in a Congressional Election," *Western Political Quarterly* (December 1975): 668-684. For an extensive analysis of the 1978 House results, see Glenn Parker, "Incumbent Popularity and Electoral Success," *Sage Electoral Studies Yearbook*, vol. 6, ed. L. Sandy Maisel and Joseph Cooper (Beverly Hills: Sage Publications, 1981).

9. See Parker, "Incumbent Popularity and Electoral Success." The 1978 questions were asked only for the House. The one National Election Study to include Senate open-ended questions (in 1974) did not ask them for the House. Also, the 1968 Comparative State Election Project— reported in Wright, *Electoral Choice in America,* and in Hinckley et al., "Information and the Vote"—asked questions for the Senate and not the House.

10. Richard Fenno, *Home Style* (Boston: Little, Brown & Co., 1978). For this discussion, see pp. 54-61.

11. The following discussion is based on Hinckley, "House Reelections and Senate Defeats." Note that none of the specific support questions asked for House incumbents were asked for Senate incumbents.

12. Ibid. The relationships were tested controlling for the respondent's party identification.

13. Thermometer ratings provide a summary evaluation of candidates—overall how one "feels" about them, whatever the reasons or weighting of reasons contributing to the evaluation. For use of this measure, see Thomas Mann, *Unsafe At Any Margin* (Washington, D.C.: American Enterprise Institute, 1978).

14. A number of studies stress that the incumbent's advantage is not merely a matter of name recognition. See Abramowitz, "Name Recognition, Reputa-

tion, and the Incumbency Effect," and John Ferejohn, "On the Decline of Competition in Congressional Elections," *American Political Science Review* (March 1977): 166-176. For one study analyzing the interaction between the incumbent's popularity and the challenger's visibility, see Lyn Ragsdale, "Incumbent Popularity and Challenger Invisibility," *Legislative Studies Quarterly* (May 1981).

15. See Hinckley, "House Reelections and Senate Defeats."

16. John Peters and Susan Welch, "The Effects of Charges of Corruption on Voting Behavior in Congressional Elections," *American Political Science Review* (September 1980): 697-708.

17. The figures are based on the unofficial 1980 vote returns reported in *Congressional Quarterly Weekly Report*, November 8, 1980, pp. 3338-3345. The 284 incumbents winning by at least 60 percent of the vote include those winning in uncontested races.

4

The Effects of Party

The role of political parties has figured prominently in the study of American elections. Writers have shown the influence of partisanship on the vote, examined how parties affect the information and perceptions that voters hold about the candidates, and speculated about the "decline" of party voting. Party identification has been a major variable used to explain the vote and an important control variable: that is, an influence that must be identified and controlled before other influences can be examined. Few studies can be conducted without first separating out the party effects. What has held for presidential elections holds for congressional and other elections as well. Party, like incumbency, affects the congressional vote. Indeed, the impact of each factor can be seen most clearly only when one understands the impact of the other.

THE CONCEPT OF PARTY IDENTIFICATION

Basic to understanding the effects of party is the concept of *party identification*. Put simply, a majority of Americans—currently about 60 percent—tend to identify with one of the two major political parties and to use that identification when they cast their vote. They think of themselves as Republicans or Democrats. This self-identification is what is meant by party identification. Political scientists are studying the different forms this influence can take and the different ways it can be measured.[1] Nevertheless, most would agree generally on its importance.

Table 4-1 shows the distribution of party identification during a quarter of a century of American politics. People who identify themselves as Democrats or Republicans are further distinguished as to whether they are strong Democrats or Republicans or not so strong.

Independents are distinguished as to whether they say they lean toward either party or not. One can see from the table the stability of party identification over time. But one can also see the rise in the ranks of all Independents—from an average of 25 percent during the 1960s, to a high of 41 percent in 1974, and down slightly to 37 percent in 1978. One finds also that the Democrats have the edge: more people are willing to call themselves Democrats than Republicans. This Democratic advantage in party identification has major implications, as we will see, for the composition of the membership elected to Congress.

Party identification appears to influence the vote in any one election, across time, and across a number of different offices. So we find "Democratic" states or districts or "Republican" states or districts that tend to vote for their party's candidates or at least give them more votes because they have more identifiers from one party than other states and districts. A Republican landslide election may produce a 65 percent margin for a Republican candidate in a Republican state or a 49 percent margin in a strongly Democratic state. Both have swung decidedly for the Republican candidate, but they have done so from their own very different bases in party identification.

Party identification, a number of writers suggest, also acts as a "perceptual screen," affecting citizens' selection of information about politics and their perception of the candidates. People pick up favorable perceptions about the candidates of their own party and screen out favorable perceptions about the opposing party's candidates. Depending on one's party and other group identifications, one talks to different people, reads different newspapers or no newspapers at all. Thus we find the situation portrayed in the political cartoon where the citizen says proudly, "Me, I vote the *man,* not the party—Eisenhower, Nixon, Ford, Reagan. . . ."

The influence of party can be understood in terms of the selection process outlined in Chapter 1. Faced with limits on time, information, and interest, voters can apply a general rule to simplify and shorten the process of decision. Party supplies such a general rule. A person may have read or heard little about the candidates but is automatically supplied with party labels on the ballot along with the names of the candidates. Partisans can assume that the candidates of their own party will be better able to represent people like themselves than would candidates of another party. It follows that such a general rule can be applied over time and across a number of political offices. Generally speaking, the best bet, the voter assumes, for choosing the candidate closest to one's ideal choice is to choose in accord with party identification.

Of course, people may happen to vote for their own party's candidates for entirely different reasons. They may be voting for the

Table 4-1 Distribution of Party Identification in the United States, 1952-1978 (Percentage of Sample)

	1952	1954	1956	1958	1960	1962	1964	1966	1968	1970	1972	1974	1976	1978
Strong Democrat	22	22	21	23	21	23	26	18	20	20	15	18	15	15
Democrat	25	25	23	24	25	23	25	27	25	23	25	21	25	24
Independent Democrat	10	9	7	7	8	8	9	9	10	10	11	13	12	14
Independent	5	7	9	8	8	8	8	12	11	13	13	15	14	14
Independent Republican	7	6	8	4	7	6	6	7	9	8	11	9	10	9
Republican	14	14	14	16	13	16	13	15	14	15	13	14	14	13
Strong Republican	13	13	15	13	14	12	11	10	10	10	10	8	9	8
Don't Know; No Answer	4	4	3	5	4	4	2	2	1	1	2	3	1	3
Total	100%	100%	100%	100%	100%	100%	100%	100%	100%	100%	100%	101%	100%	100%
(N)	1614	1139	1772	1269	3021	1289	1571	1291	1553	1802	2705	1528	2872	2304

* Less than one percent.

SOURCE: *Leadership and Change* by Warren E. Miller and Teresa E. Levitin, p. 36. Copyright © 1976. Reprinted by permission of Winthrop Publishers, Inc., Cambridge, Massachusetts. 1976 and 1978 results were calculated by the author from the 1976 and 1978 National Election Study, Center for Political Studies, University of Michigan. 1974 figures corrected by Center for Political Studies, University of Michigan.

incumbent or for a candidate preferred after a long and detailed study of qualifications and issues. Neither surveys nor aggregate-level results can easily separate these voters from others who also vote along party lines.

PARTY AND CONGRESSIONAL VOTING

The Impact of Party

The implications for congressional voting are clear and important. Partisanship affects the ability to recall the name of the candidate and to make comments about the candidate. People are more likely to recall the name and say something about their own party's candidates than about those of the opposing party.[2] Visibility may not produce positive effects, but the lack of visibility can reduce the likelihood that a candidate is voted for. Independently of visibility, partisanship also affects the evaluation of candidates and the rating of the incumbent's job performance. Finally, as might be expected from the effects on visibility and evaluations, partisanship affects the vote.

An illustration of these effects is provided in Table 4-2. People's rating of the incumbent's job performance varies with their partisanship and so does their voting behavior. Whereas 79 percent of the self-identified strong Democrats think the Democratic House incumbent is doing a good job, only 54 percent of the strong Republicans think so. The mirror image is seen for Republican incumbents, with 58 percent of strong Democrats giving them a good job rating compared to 84 percent of the strong Republicans. The same pattern is found for the feeling thermometer ratings and statements about liking and disliking the candidates, although these are not shown in the table. The behavioral result of these perceptions is the act of voting, shown in the final column of Table 4-2. As one moves from strong Democrats through Independents to strong Republicans, the proportion voting for Democratic House candidates falls sharply and consistently from 87 percent for strong Democrats to 20 percent for strong Republicans.

The comparison with the Democratic presidential incumbent at the time is worth noting. As the table makes clear, Carter is rated less highly overall than Democratic representatives, but the effects of partisanship are the same. Whereas 56 percent of strong Democrats would give the president a good job rating, only 16 percent of the strong Republicans would do so. The range is greater for the presidential job performance than for the House performance ratings. Partisans, evidently, differ more sharply about their presidents' performance than their representatives'. Nevertheless, they differ in the same way—predictably by party—for both presidential and congressional voting. The pattern shown here for 1978 could be seen for a number of other years and other political offices.

KISHA
KELLY
ANAN
ERNEST
JESSR
TRISHA
OLGA
OLGA
JULIA
KOLEEN
DOLRES
VIRGINA
KATHY
LYNDA
GILBERT
MARIA
RAFEL
PAM
GERRI
CLAUDIA
MISTY
MONICA
DANA

50% Off

ORIGINAL PRICE

L-XL

Table 4-2 Party Identification, Job Performance Ratings, and the House Vote

Party Identification	Percent of Respondents Giving Good Job Ratings[1]						Percent of Voters[2] Voting for Democratic House Candidates	
	Democratic Incumbent		Republican Incumbent		Democratic Presidential Incumbent (Carter)			
	N	%	N	%	N	%	N	%
Strong Democrat	(194)	79	(69)	58	(333)	56	(200)	87
Democrat	(275)	66	(124)	54	(539)	40	(210)	80
Independent Democrat	(136)	60	(89)	55	(321)	42	(129)	62
Independent	(114)	61	(85)	66	(294)	32	(98)	57
Independent Republican	(97)	62	(70)	78	(210)	21	(109)	38
Republican	(105)	54	(105)	70	(282)	17	(146)	34
Strong Republican	(78)	54	(73)	84	(176)	16	(115)	20
Total	(999)	64%	(615)	65%	(2155)	35%	(1007)	59%

[1] Based on all respondents in the 1978 sample who could answer the questions. The percent is the proportion of respondents in the category who gave the incumbents either good or very good job ratings. For example, of the 194 strong Democrats from districts with a Democratic incumbent, 79 percent gave the incumbent good or very good job ratings. Of the 69 strong Democrats in districts with a Republican incumbent, 58 percent gave the incumbent good or very good ratings.

[2] Based on all voters in the sample who could answer the questions. The percent is the proportion of respondents in the category who said that they voted for the Democratic House candidate, whether incumbent, challenger or open-seat candidate. For example, of the 200 strong Democrats in the sample who said that they voted, 87 percent voted for a Democratic candidate.

SOURCE: Warren Miller and Jack Katosh, "Design and Core Data for the 1978 Election Study," in *Sage Electoral Studies Yearbook*, vol. 6, ed. L. Sandy Maisel and Joseph Cooper (Beverly Hills: Sage Publications, 1981), adapted from Tables 1-7, 3-3, and 4-1, originally compiled from data from the 1978 National Election Study.

The Limits of Party

The limits as well as the strengths of party voting need some attention. By the end of the 1970s, almost 40 percent of Americans surveyed said that they did not identify with a party, and 14 percent said that they did not even lean toward a party. The identifiers themselves, as we saw in Table 4-2, often defect and vote for a candidate of the opposing party. According to the table, nearly 20 percent of Democratic identifiers and more than 20 percent of Republicans in 1978 voted for the opposing party's candidate. These trends appear to have been increasing in recent years. We find (1) a decreasing number of party identifiers, (2) increasing defection rates among the remaining partisans, and (3) a corresponding increase in "split-ticket" voting among both Independents and partisans: i.e the vote for candidates of different parties for two or more offices at the same election.

Many writers see these trends as part of a general decline in the importance of party at both nomination and electoral levels. Walter Dean Burnham, for example, speaks of the increasing defection and rise of a new breed of informed, issue-oriented Independents as part of a trend whereby "political parties are progressively losing their hold upon the electorate." Burnham sees an "onward march toward electoral

Table 4-3   Partisan Defection in House and Presidential Elections (In Percentages)

	House Elections			Presidential Elections		
	Party Voters	Defectors	Independents	Party Voters	Defectors	Independents
1956	82	9	9	76	15	9
1958	84	11	5			
1960	80	12	8	79	13	8
1962	83	12	6			
1964	79	15	5	79	15	5
1966	76	16	8			
1968	74	19	7	69	23	9
1970	76	16	8			
1972	75	17	8	67	25	8
1974	74	18	8			
1976	72	19	9	74	15	11
1978	69	22	9			

SOURCE: Thomas Mann and Raymond Wolfinger, "Candidates and Parties in Congressional Elections," *American Political Science Review* (September 1980): 620, Table 2. © 1980 by American Political Science Association. Reprinted by permission.

NOTE: Party voters are those who voted for the party with which they identified, and defectors those who voted against the party. Independents who say they lean toward one party or the other are treated as partisans in this analysis.

Table 4-4 Defection Rates for House Incumbents and Challengers (In Percentages)

	Incumbent Partisans N	%	Challenger Partisans N	%
1958	(406)	9	(291)	16
1960	(534)	8	(394)	19
1962	**		**	
1964	(430)	11	(311)	25
1966	(296)	9	(200)	33
1968	(355)	14	(286)	33
1970	(253)	5	(190)	32
1972	(323)	6	(168)	56
1974	(255)	13	(181)	49

** Data not available.

SOURCE: Albert Cover, "One Good Term Deserves Another," *American Journal of Political Science* (August 1977): 535. © 1977 by University of Texas Press. Reprinted by permission.

disaggregation" leading to "the gradual disappearance of the political party in the United States."[3] However, since this kind of prediction has relied heavily on presidential voting results, a closer look at congressional defections is necessary.

The surface pattern of defections in House and presidential voting is presented in Table 4-3. Party identifiers in the table include those Independents who say they lean toward either of the two major parties. As the table makes clear, defection among party identifiers voting for House candidates has increased from 1956 to 1978. Indeed, House defections may be in the process of surpassing the presidential defection rates. In 1976, 15 percent of party identifiers defected in their vote for president, and 19 percent defected in their vote for the House, followed by 22 percent in 1978.[4]

We need to look, however, beyond the surface pattern of defections to the effects of incumbency discussed in Chapter 3. The advantage of incumbency has also been increasing during this period, and the party defections may be votes for the incumbent of the opposing party. *Partisan weakness may be incumbency strength.* This indeed is the case as can be shown by Table 4-4. The table distinguishes between identifiers of the incumbent's party and identifiers of the challenger's party and then reports the respective rates. While incumbent partisans show no clear defection trend, challenger partisans have increasingly defected since 1958, until by 1972 about half had left their party's congressional candidate to vote for the incumbent. Albert Cover summarizes the results:

In a sense partisan identification is now a meaningless voting cue for these [challenger] partisans in congressional elections. They are as likely to support the incumbent candidate as they are the candidate of their own party. From a different perspective their partisan identification does have an impact; it prevents them from supporting the incumbent as overwhelmingly as do those belonging to the incumbent's party. Still, when one's partisan decision rule amounts to tossing a fair coin in the voting booth, it is not unreasonable to assert that the ties of partisanship are very tenuous indeed.[5]

This fact, not well recognized in the literature, must be understood: the widely noted increase in party defections in House elections can be primarily attributed to the influence of incumbency.

Both party and incumbency provide "low-cost" information cues to people facing a voting decision. The candidate's party is supplied on the ballot. The incumbent's name and generally positive reputation are known. Either may be used with little expenditure of time and effort in information-gathering—and either one may be substituted for the other. The same substitution is seen for the Senate from 1948 to 1970: as the influence of party decreases the influence of incumbency grows. The

Table 4-5   Party and Incumbency Voting in the House and Senate (Percentage of Voters)

Party Identifiers Only	House Voters (N=501)	Senate Voters (N=255)
For Party/For Incumbent	61	42
For Party/Against Incumbent	20	38
Against Party/For Incumbent	17	15
Against Party/Against Incumbent	3	6
Total	(101%)	(101%)

Party Identifiers and Independents	House Identifiers (N=501)	House Independents (N=256)	Senate Identifiers (N=255)	Senate Independents (N=140)
For Incumbent	78	80	56	69
Against Incumbent	22	20	44	31
Total	(100%)	(100%)	(100%)	(100%)

SOURCE: Computed by the author from data in the 1978 National Election Study, Center for Political Studies, University of Michigan.

NOTE: Based on all voters who identified with one of the two major parties and who voted in contests with incumbents. Party identifiers are taken to be those occupying the four extreme points on the traditional seven-party party identification scale as shown in Table 4-1: Strong Democrat, Democrat, Strong Republican, Republican. Percentages may not sum to 100 because of rounding.

pattern holds for both Republican and Democratic incumbent contests. "Incumbency now serves," concludes Warren Kostroski, "at least in Senate contests, as an important alternate voting cue to party."[6] Kostroski's analysis ends with 1970, about the time when Senate incumbency rates began to fall. It would be interesting to extend the analysis through the 1970s to see if Senate party voting gains in importance.

None of the analysis thus far directly compares House and Senate voting. We know that incumbents are more likely to be voted for in the House than in the Senate, but we do not know the relative trade-off of party and incumbency cues. To what extent in the two kinds of contests must a choice be made between the cues, and, when it is posed, which cue is selected? One such direct, if very preliminary, comparison is provided by the 1978 survey results. (See Table 4-5.) The upper portion of the table reports results for party identifiers only and the lower portion for both party identifiers and Independents.

Examining the results for party identifiers only (the upper portion of the table) yields several points of importance. First, note that party accords with incumbency more often in House than in Senate voting: House voters in the 1978 sample found fewer conflicts between the cues. Second, when a conflict is posed, House voters are more likely to defect from party than are Senate voters. In the cases of conflict, House voters divide fairly evenly between party and incumbency, while Senate voters are much more likely to follow party lines. In the House almost as many members of the challenger's party vote for the incumbent against their party as vote for their own party's candidate against the incumbent. Twenty percent vote for their party's candidate against the incumbent, while 17 percent vote for the incumbent against their party. In the Senate, 38 percent vote with the party against the incumbent, while only 15 percent vote for the incumbent against the party.

Clearly, House incumbents are advantaged—at least in the sample—at two points in the selection: first, in comparison with Senate incumbents, they face voters more compatible in terms of partisanship; and second, they are more likely to be chosen even by the opposing party voters.

A final point is also important. Note the very small numbers of party identifiers not following either party or incumbency cues. Three percent of House voters in the sample cast votes that could not be explained by partisanship or incumbency. Among Senate voters in the sample, 6 percent cast such votes. This, of course, does not mean that all other voters used a partisan or pro-incumbent rationale; many different kinds of selection could have led to the same result. It does help to underline, however, the combined importance of the two influences.

The lower portion of the table clarifies the Senate-House differences by adding Independents to the analysis. As the preceding chapter would lead us to expect, House voting for incumbents is higher than Senate voting, with the pattern holding for both Independents and identifiers. Indeed, Burnham's "new breed" of Independents are as likely to support House incumbents as the party identifiers are! Partisanship makes little difference in House voting, whereas it does make a difference in Senate voting. The Independent voters are more likely to support incumbents than the identifiers are. Nevertheless, there are a good number of Independents—31 percent—who will vote against the incumbents in the Senate. These voters also do not follow either party or incumbency cues.

Overall, the situation can be summarized as follows. Party and incumbency appear to be alternative low-cost voting cues: an increase in one is associated with a decrease in the other. However, the underlying logic of the causation is still not clear. Some writers have argued that the general decline in partisanship in American politics has led voters to search for other voting cues: hence, as party weakens, incumbency grows stronger.[7] Nevertheless, this argument, which works nicely for the House, does not account for the recent Senate results, with incumbents increasingly being defeated. Perhaps an increase of information about Senate candidates—from campaign spending or media attention—has reduced the viability of the incumbency cue. Voters have available information about two candidates. Therefore, a general decrease in party voting need not bring so automatic and predictable a change to the alternative low-information cue. Further work is needed to investigate these and other possibilities.

The Normal Vote

From the importance of party identification, we can derive the idea of a normal vote. A normal vote is an abstraction—a hypothetical vote—based on the percentage of people identifying with the two parties (plus an estimate of the likelihood that they will vote).[8] It assumes that all those who identify with a party will vote for their party's candidates and that Independents will split evenly, neither party having an advantage in the vote. In other words, the normal vote is the hypothetical vote that would occur if there were no influences beyond party—no voter decisions based on the candidates themselves or on campaign issues.

The normal vote thus provides a baseline of great value in analyzing elections. Comparing the difference between the normal vote and the actual election result, one can begin to measure the extent and direction of the various influences operating in any one election. For instance, if a normal vote—for the nation, a state, or any population or subgroup—were calculated as 54 percent Democratic, a victory for a Democratic candidate of 64 percent of the vote would show strongly pro-Democratic effects at work. Some factor, *other than party,* would be helping the Democratic candidate in that election. Similarly, if a Democratic candidate won by 50.1 percent of the vote, we should not ask why that candidate won but rather why the Republican opponent was slightly advantaged.

Analyzing Short-Term Effects. Normal vote analysis has been used primarily at the presidential level to measure "short-term" electoral effects: i.e., the influences arising from the events or candidates or issues of a particular time and situation.[9] Three important kinds of short-term influences can be identified:

- perceptions of the candidates
- perceptions of the issues
- perceptions of the parties

Candidate perceptions can affect the vote when people see one candidate, because of age or background or personal characteristics, as more "qualified," "honest," or "reliable" than the other. Issue perceptions also create short-term forces. Inflation, defense spending, abortion have been issues in recent campaigns. Party perceptions are usually shaped by the events or experience of recent presidential administrations. The Republican party was once seen negatively as the party most likely to involve the country in another depression or major recession and the Democratic party negatively as the one most likely to involve the country in another war. Presidents contribute to these party perceptions. Thus the Watergate scandal during the Nixon administration appeared to produce a short-term effect against Republican candidates.

These perceptions, of course, can contribute to a change in party identification. The issues raised by the Great Depression in the 1930s became associated with the two political parties and formed the basis for a new long-term Democratic realignment. Nevertheless, in analyzing elections these three short-term forces can be shown to be separate and independently useful in explaining or predicting results.

The normal vote for the nation in recent years has been calculated as approximately 54 percent Democratic, 46 percent Republican.[10] This means that Democrats have the edge in national elections—in voting for president and in the number of House and Senate seats they can expect to capture overall. Republicans must find or create a favorable short-term effect sufficient to overcome their deficit in the normal vote, while Democrats can win a "normal vote" election. It also means that, other things being equal, the Democrats would be expected to enjoy majority control in both the Senate and House. This is indeed the case. Since 1932, the Democrats have controlled both chambers of Congress with only three exceptions: the 80th and 83rd Congresses following the elections of 1946 and 1952, when both chambers had Republican majorities, and the 97th Congress following the 1980 election, when the Senate went narrowly Republican. (See Appendix Table A-2 on page

144.) This pattern of Democratic control, well-known to students of American politics, can be traced to the influence of partisanship in congressional elections.

Figure 4-1 shows the actual vote for presidential and House candidates against the calculated normal vote. The presidential vote swings widely pro-Republican and pro-Democratic. These swings can be seen as the result of short-term forces—the candidates, issues, and party-related perceptions in the campaign. The House vote, in contrast, holds closer to the normal vote baseline. As might be expected from the relative information available about the two kinds of contests, House voting shows less impact from short-term effects, at least at the national level. Because party influences the vote for both offices, there is a basic coordination in voting results. Republican and Democratic voting strength for both offices tend to go together. But because party is more important at the congressional level and short-term fluctuations less extreme, the president will frequently be elected from one party and the Congress controlled by the other party. From 1932 to 1982, there have been 32 years of control of both the presidency and Congress by the same party and 18 years of divided control. This fact, too, can be traced to the normal vote and the relative importance of short-term forces in presidential and House elections.

In applying the traditional presidential-level analysis to voting in congressional elections, one caution is in order. The presidential analysis assumes that voting can be explained by partisanship plus the short-term effects of the candidates themselves, campaign issues, and party perceptions. Congressional analysis also can make this assumption, but it somehow needs to address the not-so-short-term effect of incumbency. If we follow the traditional normal vote analysis, some of the short-term effects will be incumbency effects. If, on the other hand, we are interested in identifying the same short-term effects that presidential studies examine, then we must control for incumbency as well as for party.

Figure 4-1 helps clarify the situation. Note the slight pro-Democratic deviation of the House vote from the normal vote in many recent elections. Some short-term force appears to be favoring Democratic candidates at the national level, and we need to ask why this should be so. The effects of incumbency offer one explanation. Since there are more Democratic than Republican incumbents (the Democrats over time winning more elections through their advantage in party identification), any general advantage of incumbency would help the Democrats more than the Republicans.

Therefore, the traditional presidential voting equation where,

$$\text{Vote} = \begin{array}{c} \text{Party} \\ \text{ID} \end{array} + \begin{array}{c} \text{Perception} \\ \text{of Candidates} \end{array} + \begin{array}{c} \text{Perception} \\ \text{of Issues} \end{array} + \begin{array}{c} \text{Perception} \\ \text{of Parties} \end{array}$$

Figure 4-1 Democratic Percentage of the Two-Party Vote: Presidential and House Elections, 1948-1978

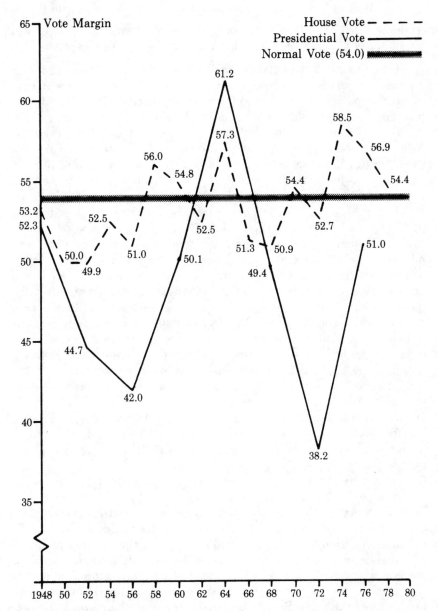

SOURCE: The Democratic percentage of the two-party vote was calculated from Democratic and Republican vote totals in *Statistics of the Presidential and Congressional Election,* biennial reports, 1948-1978, prepared by the Clerk of the House of Representatives. (According to official popular vote totals released by the Federal Election Commission on December 31, 1980, the Democratic percentage of the presidential vote in 1980 was 44.7%.)

may need adaptation in congressional analysis to

$$\text{Vote} = \frac{\text{Party}}{\text{ID}} + \text{Incumbency} + \frac{\text{Perception}}{\text{of Candidates}} + \frac{\text{Perception}}{\text{of Issues}} + \frac{\text{Perception}}{\text{of Parties}}$$

At least some attention must be given to the problem of separating incumbency effects from the other candidate-related perceptions.

Calculating a Normal Vote Without Survey Data. The same normal vote analysis can be conducted for districts or states if party identification can be calculated for these populations. This is a big "if," however, since reliable surveys that could supply information on party identification are very limited at the state and district levels. Yet, without a normal vote or some baseline measure,[11] one cannot measure the extent or direction of short-term effects. Does a very well-financed challenger losing with 47 percent of the vote do worse or better than expected? Does the support by New Right groups make a difference to an election? Do candidate characteristics such as age or sex or the particular campaign strategies adopted make a difference to the outcome? All such questions of interest to followers of elections require the measuring of short-term forces. They therefore require some baseline against which the short-term forces can be measured. Indeed, it is probably fair to say that the inability to measure short-term effects has posed the major obstacle to progress in congressional election research.

Aggregate results can be used to calculate such a baseline measure, although many difficulties beset such an analysis. In using aggregate data one can look to past results to calculate a baseline for the present. Usually, one would say, a Democratic candidate in this state or district can be expected to gain a certain share of the vote; this expected share or baseline could then be compared with the actual vote a particular Democratic candidate received. But what past results are appropriate to include? And how does one control for the short-term effects that presumably were at work in *those* elections? If one averages a large number of cases, one might expect all past short-term effect to cancel each other out. But a large number of cases appropriate for such analysis might not exist. After the national census every 10 years, House district lines are redrawn. So if one wished to calculate a baseline vote for any one district, only a short history of past results could be used for the calculation. While state lines remain the same, the analysis of Senate races raises other problems. What past results might appropriately be used for a baseline measure—the race a full six years before for the same Senate seat or other more recent state-wide results (for governor or president or the other Senate seat), all including their own short-term effects?

In spite of these problems, some cautious attempts have been made to use aggregate results to calculate baseline measures.[12] For example,

Warren Kostroski attempts to determine a minimum partisan vote for Senate candidates that might be used to measure the additional effects of incumbency or other short-term factors. He takes the minimum state-wide vote for the U.S. House races for each party across a period of five elections, arguing that the House vote may be the closest approximation to a normal vote in actual elections. The minimum vote, rather than the average vote, is selected to help limit the effects of incumbency. The minimum vote is the worst a party was able to do state-wide over a period of elections. Kostroski then applies this party vote with a measure of incumbency to assess the changing relative importance of the two influences across a number of years of Senate elections.[13]

Other analyses may find the construction of a mean state-wide House vote a more appropriate measure. Whatever the particular measure selected, one is attempting to control for the very important influence of partisanship before one can measure other effects.

SUMMARY

Many people do not pay attention to the congressional race or care much about the outcome, but they still manage to vote in the contest. We can now understand why this occurs. Both *party* and *incumbency* supply low-cost information cues to voters and help them make a general-choice decision. Both influences are strikingly apparent in the aggregate election results and are confirmed at the individual level in survey responses. Moreover, each appears to serve as an alternative to the other: as party weakens, incumbency grows stronger, and vice versa.

It is important to repeat that this need not be so: it is not merely a statistical artifact. People could, for example, vote consistently against incumbents—to supply new blood to Congress—or they could vote on issues independently of party and incumbency cues. In fact, however, very few people make such decisions, although a somewhat larger proportion do so for the Senate than for the House. While the Senate-House differences are based on only preliminary comparisons, they, too, make sense given the different levels of information about candidates in the two contests. With more information about challengers in Senate races, voters may find a vote for the incumbent less necessary or less intuitively satisfying.

There is, of course, some variation in the vote that party and incumbency cannot explain. Consider in Figure 4-1 the strong pro-Democratic effect on the House vote in 1974, the election following the Watergate investigation and the Nixon resignation. Presumably, there were short-term influences at work in that election, as well as in many other elections, that can be identified. While short-term effects appear less important in House voting than in presidential voting, they still are sufficient to swing the outcome of an election or reconstruct the majority party in the chamber. Nevertheless, only 15 percent of 1978 Senate voters, counting both party identifiers and Independents, cast votes not in accord with party or incumbency cues. Only 9 percent of House voters did the same. Indeed, when other major influences on the vote are identified—such as attitudes about the candidates or the issues—they tend to accord with party or incumbency or both. This fact will become clear in the following chapter. In other words, once party and incumbency influences are identified, there is not much variation left to explain.

NOTES

1. A good summary of the meaning and measurement of party identification is provided by Herbert Asher in *Presidential Elections and American Politics* (Homewood, Ill.: Dorsey Press, 1976), pp. 49-85. For a discussion of the current controversies, see Richard Niemi and Herbert Weisberg, *Controversies in American Voting Behavior* (San Francisco: W. H. Freeman & Co., 1976).
2. See Gary Jacobson, *Money in Congressional Elections* (New Haven: Yale University Press, 1980), pp. 18, 19. Similar results are found in House and Senate voting using the 1978 survey results.
3. Walter Dean Burnham, *Critical Elections and the Mainsprings of American Politics* (New York: W. W. Norton & Co., 1970), pp. 119-134.
4. For discussion, see Thomas Mann and Raymond Wolfinger, "Candidates and Parties in Congressional Elections," *American Political Science Review* (September 1980): 617-632.
5. Albert Cover, "One Good Term Deserves Another," *American Journal of Political Science* (August 1977): 535, 536. See also Candice Nelson, "The Effect of Incumbency on Voting in Congressional Elections, 1964-1974," *Political Science Quarterly* (Winter 1978): 665-678.
6. Warren Kostroski, "Party and Incumbency in Postwar Senate Elections," *American Political Science Review* (December 1973): 1233. For the same point, see Cover, "One Good Term Deserves Another"; Nelson, "The Effect of Incumbency"; and Barbara Hinckley et al., "Information and the Vote: A Comparative Election Study," *American Politics Quarterly* (April 1974): 131-158. In all of these studies, note that party and incumbency need not necessarily act as substitutes one for the other. Other factors also could affect the vote.
7. See Cover, "One Good Term Deserves Another," and Kostroski, "Party and Incumbency."
8. Philip Converse, "The Concept of the Normal Vote," in *Elections and the Political Order*, ed. Angus Campbell et al. (New York: John Wiley & Sons, 1966), pp. 9-40.
9. For examples of normal vote analysis, see selections in Campbell et al., *Elections and the Political Order;* Richard Boyd, "Popular Control of Public Policy: A Normal Vote Analysis of the 1968 Elections," *American Political Science Review* (June 1972): 429-449; and Arthur Miller et al., "A Majority Party in Disarray: Policy Polarization in the 1972 Elections," *American Political Science Review* (September 1976): 753-778. A good discussion is

provided in Arthur Miller, "Normal Vote Analysis: Sensitivity to Change Over Time," *American Journal of Political Science* (May 1979): 406-425.

10. Warren Miller and Teresa Levitin, *Leadership and Change* (Cambridge, Mass.: Winthrop Publishers, 1976), p. 43. See also Miller, "Normal Vote Analysis," p. 423.

11. The term *normal vote* in this discussion is used specifically to refer to the estimation of partisan forces, as derived from data on party identification. The term *baseline vote* can refer to any calculation of a hypothetical vote, however derived, that deliberately excludes short-term forces, and so by comparing the actual vote with the baseline calculation allows the short-term effects to be measured.

12. For illustrations, see Robert Erikson, "The Advantage of Incumbency in Congressional Elections," *Polity* (Spring 1971): 395-405; Gerald Wright, "Constituency Response to Congressional Behavior," *Western Political Quarterly* (September 1977): 401-410; and Harvey Kabaker, "Estimating the Normal Vote in Congressional Elections," *Midwest Journal of Political Science* (February 1969): 58-83.

13. Kostroski, "Party and Incumbency," pp. 1213-1234.

5

The Candidates

We can now turn to other influences on congressional voting — the qualifications of candidates and the issues of the campaign. These factors make the news and form the substance for the election commentaries. They are, for many people, what elections are all about. One hardly expects headlines proclaiming "Incumbent Wins Again" or "Many Voters Follow Party Lines," even if such influences must first be understood before any others can be measured.

This chapter treats an influence on congressional voting commonly assumed to be one of the most important — the qualifications of the candidates themselves. Although the subject deserves much more attention, it has been given very little study. The material that is available can be summarized briefly. We will look first at the evidence for the influence of candidate qualifications, then consider the limits on this influence, and turn finally to some unanswered, and unasked, questions.

THE CANDIDATES AND THE VOTERS

Perceptions of the Candidates

We know from surveys that candidate qualifications appear to be important: at least they are cited more frequently than remarks about issues or parties as reasons for liking or disliking the candidates in a contest. Comments about the candidates' qualifications, and particularly personal comments, predominate in House races. In the 1978 study, personal characteristics are by far the most frequently cited reason for liking or disliking House candidates — whether incumbents or challengers or candidates in open-seat races.[1] People speak of a candidate's "honesty," "sincerity," "fairness," and "dedication." The more clearly political traits of "experience" and "ability" are cited frequently for incumbents, less frequently for challengers or open-seat candidates. Altogether, however, the House pattern is clear: there is a predominant emphasis on candidate traits, both personal and political, and especially an emphasis on personal traits.

House candidates, according to Richard Fenno, attempt to communicate generalized notions of trust and competence.[2] These communications, indeed, appear to be received by the voters. Incumbents may succeed at this best: after all, they have the experience, the years making visits home, and the time accumulated to engender trust. Many challengers, of course, do not succeed in communicating anything. Nevertheless, all House candidates — to the extent that they are perceived at all — are perceived in these personal terms.

The House results can be compared with those for the Senate and for other offices.[3] Table 5-1 reports the frequency of comments about candidates, parties, and issues, with the references to candidates further divided into personal references and the more political references to experience and ability. As the table makes clear, in Senate races, too, the qualifications of candidates appear important; in particular, comments about the candidates' experience and ability are heard frequently. These are the most frequently cited references for both Democratic and Republican candidates for the Senate in 1968 and 1974. The personal characteristics so important in the House are relatively less important for the Senate, while issue and party comments are relatively more important. In the 1968 Senate races, in fact, issues comprise roughly one-quarter of all positive and negative references. It is also worth noting the negative party references to Senate Republican candidates in the Watergate election of 1974. In citing what they like and dislike about candidates, voters apparently can respond to actual political events.

These congressional responses can be compared with those for candidates for governor and president. The same people in 1968 were asked what they liked and disliked about candidates for senator, governor, and president. Issues, it appears, are cited more frequently in gubernatorial races than in Senate races by the same state-wide voters, while personal characteristics are cited less frequently for governor than for senator.[4] It is possible that the single executive head of a state is held more responsible for policy by voters than a legislator who is merely one out of one hundred members. References to the experience and ability of the candidates appear about the same in gubernatorial and Senate races. Overall, however, the Senate races would seem to have more in common with gubernatorial and presidential contests than with races for the House. Issues, party ties, experience and ability, and the personal characteristics of candidates — all capture some share of the voters' attention. In House races, however, there is less of a mixture and differentiation of responses. As Table 5-1 makes clear, of all races for major elective office, personal characteristics predominate in House races alone.

Table 5-1 Likes and Dislikes About Candidates (Percentage of References)

	Experience/ Ability	Personal Qualities	Issues/ Group Ties	Party Ties	Total
Senate 1968					
Positive D	36	19	28	16	(100%)
Positive R	41	24	22	13	(100%)
Negative D	25	26	27	20	(100%)
Negative R	18	31	26	25	(100%)
Senate 1974					
Positive D	35	29	19	17	(100%)
Positive R	41	21	19	18	(100%)
Negative D	22	32	32	14	(100%)
Negative R	17	28	20	35	(100%)
Governor 1968					
Positive D	31	17	34	18	(100%)
Positive R	40	21	25	14	(100%)
Negative D	23	25	28	23	(100%)
Negative R	19	16	34	31	(100%)
President 1968					
Positive D	33	26	31	11	(100%)
Positive R	30	27	35	8	(100%)
Negative D	23	31	29	17	(100%)
Negative R	25	39	25	11	(100%)
House 1978					
Positive D	24	60	12	4	(100%)
Positive R	28	49	19	4	(100%)
Negative D	19	46	18	18	(100%)
Negative R	14	46	13	27	(100%)

SOURCE: The 1968 results are adapted from Gerald Wright, *Electoral Choice in America* (Chapel Hill: Institute for Research in Social Science, 1974), p. 60. The 1974 and 1978 results are calculated by the author from data in the 1974 and 1978 National Election Studies, Center for Political Studies, University of Michigan.

NOTE: The table should be read as follows: for example, references to experience and ability constituted 36 percent of all positive (liked) responses to Democratic Senate candidates in 1968.

Of course, voters' comments about the candidates are very general. This has been observed for a number of years and in both Senate and House contests. Donald Stokes and Warren Miller summarize House responses in the 1950s as "a collection of diffuse evaluative judgments." People commented that a candidate was "experienced," "knew the problems," "was a good man," or "had done a good job."[5] The same observations were made for the House in 1978 and the Senate in 1968. In the 1968 study, the most general comments were by far the most frequently cited. People liked or disliked the candidate's "record," liked someone's "experience," or saw one candidate (usually the incumbent) as the "lesser evil" of the two. The known incumbent was perceived to be a lesser evil than the unknown challenger.[6] Yet it is important to see that in some contests fairly specific information does get across to voters. In 1968, for example, the most frequent negative comment about Republican incumbents concerned their advanced age (with 10 percent of the responses in this category). Other specific references included positive comments about the natural resource policy of Democratic incumbents (5 percent of responses), negative comments about the liberalism of Democratic challengers (3 percent), and negative comments about Democratic incumbents' older age (3 percent).[7]

Not only can voters say why they like or dislike candidates, but in both Senate and House contests these likes and dislikes are significantly related to the vote. One study compares a number of influences for their effect on the vote: the likes and dislikes, separated in terms of the four categories shown in Table 5-1; the voter's party identification; and whether there is a Republican incumbent, a Democratic incumbent, or no incumbent in the race. For the 1978 House races, the personal qualities of candidates have the greatest impact, followed by party identification and incumbency. The experience and ability of candidates rank fourth in impact, stronger than either issues or party ties. For the 1974 Senate races, the candidate's experience and ability are surpassed only by the effects of party identification. Personal qualities are third in impact and stronger than issues, party ties, or incumbency.[8] In other words, the voter's perception of the candidates does indeed influence the vote independently of the effects of partisanship and incumbency.

Candidate Preference, Party, and Incumbency

Nevertheless, there are limits to what the candidate preferences of voters can explain. Richard Brody has proposed that potential voters follow *two decision rules:* first and primarily, they decide which candidate is preferred; and second, if neither is preferred, they follow party identification. (With no candidate preferred and no party identification, the potential voters abstain.) The rule holds no matter how much or how little one candidate is preferred or even if the preferred candidate is

Table 5-2   Party Identification, Candidate Preference, and Predicted Vote

Candidate Preferred*	Party Identification		
	Incumbent's Party	Independent	Challenger's Party
Incumbent	A Incumbent	B Incumbent	C Incumbent
None	D Incumbent	E Abstain	F Challenger
Challenger	G Challenger	H Challenger	I Challenger

* Based on feeling thermometer ratings.

SOURCE: Thomas Mann, *Unsafe At Any Margin* (Washington, D.C.: American Enterprise Institute, 1978), p. 64. © 1978 by American Enterprise Institute. Mann follows the decision rules suggested by Richard Brody, "Communications," *American Political Science Review* (September 1976): 924.

rated unfavorably. Preference, suggests Brody, can be measured by the feeling thermometer ratings.[9] In this formulation, candidate evaluations pose an alternative influence to party identification, capable of overriding it in deciding the vote. Table 5-2 depicts a schematic representation of the Brody model with the cells showing the predicted vote.[10]

The model, adapted for the problem of candidates who are unknown or unrateable, has been applied by Thomas Mann and Ray Wolfinger to 1978 House voting.[11] People who do not recognize or cannot rate a candidate are treated as neutral toward the candidate and scored as 50 degrees on the feeling thermometer. Thus a voter who does not know the challenger and rates the incumbent lower than 50 degrees is coded as preferring the challenger. The results for those contests between incumbents and challengers are shown in Table 5-3. Independents in the table include only those who do not lean toward one party or the other; the partisan leaners are treated as party identifiers.

While Mann and Wolfinger contend that the table supports the applicability of the candidate-preference model for congressional voting,[12] the actual results are fairly mixed. According to the *first decision rule of candidate preference,* when preference and partisanship conflict (cells C and G), people should vote for the candidate preferred. Yet while 84 percent of the challenger's partisans followed this rule, of the incumbent's partisans only 59 percent did. In other words, most people who do not follow party lines are voting for the incumbent. Independents do tend to vote for the candidate preferred by the thermometer ratings (cells B and H). According to the *second decision rule of partisanship,* when no candidate is preferred by people who can identify with a party (cells D and F), people should vote along party lines. While people of the incumbent's party vote in line with the prediction 95 percent of the time, people of the challenger's party support the prediction only 53 percent of the time. In short, the "errors" in the model's predictions consistently involve votes for the incumbent that were expected to go to the challenger.

These results can be cited to show that the candidates make a difference to the vote—that specific candidate traits are important. Yet, the thermometer ratings tell us which candidates are preferred; they do

Table 5-3 Party Identification, Candidate Preference, and Reported Vote, House 1978 (N=757)

| Candidate Preferred | *Percentage Following the Model's Prediction*[1] Party Identification[2] | | |
	Incumbent's Party	Independent	Challenger's Party
Incumbent	A 99% Incumbent (N=260)	B 91% Incumbent (N=34)	C 84% Incumbent (N=123)
None	D 95% Incumbent (N=130)	E ----[3] Abstain (N=31)	F 53% Challenger (N=95)
Challenger	G (59%) Challenger (N=17)	H (86%) Challenger (N=7)	I 97% Challenger (N=60)

[1] The percentage is the proportion of the total vote that accords with the prediction. The prediction from Table 5-2 is included in the cell. Thus in cell F, 53 percent of the 95 voters supported the challenger in line with the prediction and 47 percent supported the incumbent against the prediction. Percentages based on N's of less than 25 are reported in parentheses.

[2] Independents include only those who say they do not lean toward a party.

[3] The prediction is not to vote. 81 percent of those voting supported the incumbent.

SOURCE: Adapted from Thomas Mann and Raymond Wolfinger, "Candidates and Parties in Congressional Elections," *American Political Science Review* (September 1980): 625, Table 9. © 1980 by American Political Science Association. Reprinted by permission.

Table 5-4   Alternative Explanations of Congressional Voting[1]

Decision Rules	N	Percentage of Cases Unexplained
Candidate Preference or Party[2]	(726)	8
Incumbency or Party	(757)	4
Candidate Preference or Party or Incumbency	(757)	2

[1] Based on the results from Table 5-3. Independent leaners are included here with party identifiers, in contrast to earlier Table 4-5.

[2] Omitting the cases where neither candidate preference nor party affiliation is reported. These 31 cases, of voters who were predicted to abstain by the candidate-preference model, could also be counted as votes unexplained. If this were done, the percent of 757 cases would be 12% unexplained.

not tell us why. A rating is itself a kind of vote, in need of explanation. Perhaps the most interesting fact from Table 5-3 is supplied by the N's in parentheses: very few people, even among members of the challenger's party, preferred the challenger to the incumbent. (Recall from the thermometer ratings in Chapter 3 that even when challengers could be rated, they tended to receive neutral 50 degree scores.) This fact leads back to the complex of factors supporting incumbents discussed in Chapters 2 and 3. One can argue that the candidates preferred, who often happen to be incumbents, will be voted for. But why are House incumbents so consistently preferred? And what accounts for the cases in Table 5-3 where people predicted to vote for the challenger vote for the incumbent?

Consider the following two explanations of congressional voting. First, modifying Brody's model, one could specify two equally weighted decision rules: people will either vote for the candidate preferred or vote in accord with their party affiliation. Alternatively, given the low interest in and information about congressional races, people may decide to apply a general rule: either the general rule of voting for the incumbent or the general rule of voting with their party affiliation. Table 5-4 compares the results from Table 5-3 for these two different explanations.

The modified candidate-preference model, relaxed to allow either candidate preference or party to explain the vote, leaves 8 percent of the cases unexplained. The general-choice model, specifying merely a vote by party or incumbency, leaves only 4 percent of the cases unexplained. *Simply knowing the party of the incumbent is an even better predictor of results than knowing which candidate is preferred.* The three rules together (of candidate preference or party or incumbency) can "explain" all but 2 percent of the results. These remaining cases may well represent a core of idiosyncratic voters (or idiosyncratic responders to survey questions) that no further analysis could explain. But if the best one could do is leave 2 percent of the cases unexplained, then it is noteworthy that applying merely the general rules about party and incumbency to House voting explains all but 4 percent.

The results this far suggest that voters vote for the candidates they like best—not a very surprising finding. But the liking itself tends to follow partisanship and, in the House at least, the cue of incumbency. Congressional candidates, remember, are rarely disliked: a neutral rating on the thermometer scale is sufficient to lose in the voting decision. At times, then, the "candidate preferred" will simply be the one able to transmit some information to the voters. Moreover, this liking tends to be expressed in general terms, with few specific traits given by way of explanation. One can argue, therefore, that people vote for the candidates they like; but one cannot argue, at least on the evidence to date, that they have weighed any specific qualifications of the two candidates to reach this decision.

SPECIFIC CANDIDATE TRAITS

These studies, however, show one side only—the voters' perception. We still do not know if qualifications possessed by the candidates or emphasized in the campaign are transmitted to the voters. Until we have linked the information transmitted and the information received, we know little about the impact of candidate characteristics on congressional election results.

Many characteristics usually thought to be politically important—age, sex, ethnic background, religion—may not be tapped by the survey questions. These traits might affect someone's perception of competence or trustworthiness, but we could not deduce this from the survey responses. We would simply know that one candidate was better liked, more trusted, or rated higher on the feeling thermometers than another. Some characteristics may become important in certain circumstances and not in others. In some contests, a candidate's age or leadership in Congress might become a negative campaign issue, whereas in other contests with candidates of the identical age or leadership status nothing is heard of the issue. Some effect of the campaign, rather than the characteristic itself, would appear critical. Finally, some candidate traits may be most important at stages other than the electoral one. Earlier stages of a recruitment process—with state party activists or interest group leaders—may select those candidate characteristics between which the voters will "choose." Clearly, a fuller understanding of the impact of candidate characteristics will require work with contextual and aggregate results.

Age

The age of candidates is often considered a decisive factor in the outcome of a contest: thus the defeat of a Senate incumbent is often attributed to the candidate's advanced age. Of course, many very elderly incumbents can also be re-elected, although they do not become cited. Is there, in fact, any discernible effect of age, and in particular, of advanced age, on electoral outcomes? We can look to the many Senate incumbents losing elections in recent years and ask if the age of the incumbent, the age of the challenger, or the relative effect of both ages makes any difference to the results.

Table 5-5 lists losing incumbents only, with their age, number of years in the Senate, and the age of the victorious challenger. Focusing only on these election upsets suggests that age might be important. With the significant exception of the race in California, where a 70-year-old challenger beat a 42-year-old incumbent, it appears that many younger challengers have beaten older incumbents. There are many "examples"

Table 5-5   Age and Election Defeat: Senate Incumbent Losers, 1974-1978

Incumbent	Age	Years In Senate	Challenger's Age
1974			
Dominick (R-Colo.)	59	12	36
Cook (R-Ky.)	48	6	50
1976			
Tunney (D-Calif.)	42	6	70
Hartke (D-Ind.)	57	18	59
Beall (R-Md.)	49	6	43
Montoya (D-N.M.)	61	12	41
Buckley (C/R-N.Y.)	53	6	49
Taft (R-Ohio)	59	6	59
Brock (R-Tenn.)	45	6	45
Moss (D-Utah)	65	18	42
McGee (D-Wyo.)	61	18	43
1978			
Haskell (D-Colo.)	62	6	41
Clark (D-Iowa)	49	6	49
Hathaway (D-Maine)	54	6	38
Brooke (R-Mass.)	59	12	37
Griffin (R-Mich.)	55	12	44
McIntyre (D-N.H.)	63	18	37

SOURCE: Calculated by the author.

NOTE: The age used is the age at the time of defeat.

Table 5-6 Age and Election Defeat: Senate Winners and Losers, 1974-1978

	N	Age (Mean Years)	Percentage Younger Than Incumbents
Incumbents			
Winning	(54)[1]	56.8	—
Losing	(17)	55.4	—
Challengers			
Winning	(17)	46.1[2]	65%
Losing	(48)	44.7	69%

[1] Six incumbents faced no major party opposition. Thus there are 54 winning incumbents and 48 losing challengers.

[2] Based on the 16 cases omitting the 70-year-old challenger S. I. Hayakawa, the mean age would be 44.6 years.

SOURCE: Calculated by the author.

that could be cited. At the same time, however, it is notable that a number of incumbents in their forties (a young age for the Senate) are defeated as well as a number who are seeking their first re-election. Moreover, in the same election years that these incumbents are losing, seven who are past the age of 65 are going on to victory.

Focusing on losers alone, in fact, gives a very misleading impression. If one compares the ages of losers and winners, as in Table 5-6, a clearer picture emerges. The age of the incumbents, the challengers, and both in combination makes no difference to the winning or losing of elections. (For the full list of Senate incumbent winners and losers, see Appendix Table A-4 on p. 147.) The two populations of winners and losers are virtually identical in age. Indeed, the very slight differences that exist are in the opposite direction: losing incumbents are on the average one year younger than winning incumbents, and winning challengers are slightly older than losing challengers. Even if one omits the 70-year-old S. I. Hayakawa in the California race, the challengers who win and the challengers who lose show no difference in age. A majority of challengers are younger than the incumbents—on the average about 10 years younger—whether they win or whether they lose.

In some races and in the perception of some voters, a senator's age may be important. It can be cited in responses to the open-ended questions. But Table 5-6 suggests that overall there is no relationship between age and losing and winning. If age is not important in itself as an influence on elections, we will need to ask why and how it can become salient in some campaigns and not in others.

Sex

Sex, like age, is often thought to have political implications. As Table 5-7 makes clear, very few women have been elected to Congress, and recent years show no increasing trend. After the 1980 election, Eleanor Smeal, president of the National Organization for Women (NOW), commented that at the present rate it would take women 217 years to reach equal representation in Congress.[13] But to what extent is this unequal representation produced electorally rather than at other points in the process of recruiting congressional candidates? Does the sex of the candidates affect election results?

One study by Robert Darcy and Sarah Schramm compares male and female House candidates for contested races from 1970 to 1974. In the 1,099 races examined, 91 women candidates participated in 87 races. Darcy and Schramm compare the percentage of the vote for male and female candidates by party and incumbency status and find very little difference between the sexes in their vote-getting ability. In the six comparisons reported in Table 5-8, only one shows any significant difference by sex, and that one favors female candidates. Democratic female incumbents, some of whom have run in very safe districts, gain larger vote totals than Democratic male incumbents. While there are some differences between the parties, with Democratic women doing relatively better compared to male candidates than Republican women, overall the results are striking for their similarities and not their differences. *The sex of the candidate makes little difference to the vote margin.*[14] Incumbents do well no matter what their sex or the sex of their

Table 5-7   Number of Women in Congress, 1953-1982

Congress	Senate	House	Congress	Senate	House
83rd	3	12	91st	1	10
84th	1	16	92nd	2	13
85th	1	15	93rd	0	16
86th	1	16	94th	0	19
87th	2	17	95th	2	18
88th	2	11	96th	1	16
89th	2	10	97th	2	19
90th	1	11			

SOURCE: Congressional Quarterly, *Members of Congress Since 1789* (Washington, D.C.: Congressional Quarterly, 1981), pp. 4, 5. The figures include women appointed to office as well as those chosen by voters in general elections and special elections. The 97th Congress figures are as of the 1980 November election. Gladys Noon Spellman is included in the House tally, although her seat in Maryland's 5th congressional district was declared vacant by the House February 24, 1981, because of disability.

Table 5-8 Vote Gained by Male and Female Candidates in House Races, 1970-1974

	Male Candidates		Female Candidates	
	N	Percent Democratic Vote	N	Percent Democratic Vote
Democratic				
Incumbents	(458)	67.7	(18)	75.1*
Challengers	(425)	39.3	(29)	37.6
Open-Seat Candidates	(124)	52.1	(10)	57.6
	N	Percent Republican Vote	N	Percent Republican Vote
Republican				
Incumbents	(425)	60.6	(6)	54.5
Challengers	(458)	32.2	(13)	29.5
Open-Seat Candidates	(124)	47.8	(7)	43.2

* Statistically significant at the .05 level. All other differences between male and female candidates are not significant at this level.

SOURCE: Adapted from Robert Darcy and Sarah Schramm, "When Women Run Against Men," *Public Opinion Quarterly* (1977): 4, 5. The data are based on all contested major-party races where male or female candidates opposed male candidates.

opponents; challengers do poorly; and open-seat candidates run more closely contested races.

Darcy and Schramm extend the study to look at individual responses to survey questions. Again, the findings are important for the lack of differences they reveal. Turnout for both male and female voters appeared unaffected by the candidacy of women. The recognition of candidates also was unaffected: the women candidates, the authors conclude, shared obscurity with the men. If there are some voters who favor or oppose women candidates, they are balanced by voters with opposing tendencies, and both groups are overwhelmed by the people with no opinions or no recognition of the candidates. On balance, then, in both the individual responses and the actual vote received, the sex of the candidates does not appear to affect the election results.

We can look to recent years for further confirmation. In the elections from 1974 through 1978, incumbent women lost only 2 of 40 bids for re-election, for a success rate of 95 percent, one very similar to the rate for House incumbents as a whole. In 1978, of the major party candidates running for their first election, 3 women won and 22 lost. The 3 who won ran in open-seat contests, and all 3 spent more than their opponents in the campaign. All of the 22 who lost ran against incumbents, with only 4 of these unsuccessful challengers gaining more than 40 percent of the vote. Only one of these 4 spent more than the incumbent.

In short, the election patterns for women closely resemble those for the House as a whole. There are, however, some points of distinction. Of the 23 women elected from 1974 through 1978, 18 were Democrats and 5 Republicans—a partisan concentration much more Democratic than the House as a whole. Nearly one-half (10 of the 23) came from only three states—Maryland, New York, and New Jersey. Indeed, in the 96th Congress, one-fourth of the women members in the House came from the state of Maryland. (See Appendix Table A-8 on page 158.)

Something occurring before the election in the politics and parties of the states appears to be influencing the selection of women for Congress.[15] The question is not whether women can win the open-seat contest, but whether they can be *nominated* for the open-seat contest, a coveted prize given the success of incumbents. In only one party primarily and in only a few Middle Atlantic states have women managed to pass this particular obstacle point in recruitment. It is not the voters, then, who are deciding whether there should be more or fewer women in Congress. Once again we are led beyond questions about voting to ask about other points in the process of selection.

These examples illustrate the very large gap between popular commentary about elections and the actual impact on the election results. According to popular accounts, age and sex (as well as other less easily measurable characteristics) are electorally relevant candidate traits, frequently cited as advantages or disadvantages in a campaign. These popular accounts also accord with the competitive view of elections in which voters weigh such specific characteristics for the two candidates in reaching their decisions. Yet, tested against the actual voting results, such specific characteristics make no difference to the vote. Whether they do so under some circumstances and not under others remains a question for future research.

Campaign Activity

"Campaign trails are well trodden but poorly mapped," Paul Dawson and James Zinser remark.[16] We have studied the *response*—in voter attitudes—but not the *stimulus* from the campaign activity or the connection, if any, between stimulus and response. Under some circumstances candidate traits may or may not become important, but we have not examined the circumstances. Candidates project their own qualifications in a campaign, emphasizing some things and de-emphasizing others. Some address their opponents' qualifications, although we do not know how many or with what success.

One set of materials is now available that can link campaign stimulus to voter response. As part of the 1978 National Election Study, literature was collected from campaign headquarters for all the districts included in the survey sample. This literature can be analyzed for the themes and emphasis of the campaign: the references to party, issues, the candidate's personal characteristics or experience, the opponent. Since the same study asks voters about their perceptions of the candidates and the race, the literature can be linked with the voter's response: for example, the likes and dislikes as reported previously in Table 5-1. We could then examine if what is communicated by the candidates is actually received by the voters and under what circumstances such communication occurs.

SUMMARY

The importance of candidate characteristics needs to be seen within the context of information affecting congressional races. Some candidates are more visible than others, while some, like many House challengers, are not visible at all. People can articulate likes and dislikes for candidates at least minimally visible and reflect these attitudes in their voting choice. Candidate liking, then, can affect the vote beyond the influence of party and incumbency. But liking the candidate does not necessarily mean that one has evaluated specific characteristics. There are limits to what the candidate-preference models can explain. For House races, simply knowing the party of the incumbent is a better predictor of the vote than knowing which candidate is preferred.

The differences in the perception of candidates are also of interest. House candidates are predominantly liked for their personal qualities although these are only very generally described. In contrast, Senate candidates are liked more for their experience and ability although references to issues, personal qualities, and party ties also figure prominently in the senatorial responses. Indeed, Senate candidates appear more like the candidates for governor and president than their congressional counterparts in the House races.

We do not yet know why these differences exist. It may be that Senate and House candidates do different things and present themselves differently to constituents and voters. Alternatively, the results may have little to do with the candidate's behavior—either in office or in the campaign. The races for senator and governor receive media attention, while most House races do not. Consequently, more information about senatorial and gubernatorial candidates is available to the voters. These races also provoke active competition, supplying voters with unfavorable information about candidates from the opponent's campaign. By this explanation, the greater differentiation of the Senate responses may be a result of the greater information available, while the House responses reflect the lack of information.

Candidate characteristics, according to the survey results, can be important to congressional voters. Yet candidates may do the same things, or be the same age, and be perceived differently. The circumstances affecting these perceptions—from the campaign and the wider political context—will need further study. Candidate characteristics can also be important to party recruiters, interest group supporters, and media commentators, and their reactions can affect and constrain what the voters decide.

NOTES

1. Glenn Parker, "Incumbent Popularity and Electoral Success," *Sage Electoral Studies Yearbook,* vol. 6, ed. L. Sandy Maisel and Joseph Cooper (Beverly Hills: Sage Publications, 1981); and Gary Jacobson, "Incumbents and Voters in the 1978 Congressional Elections," *Legislative Studies Quarterly* (May 1981).
2. Richard Fenno, *Home Style: House Members in Their Districts* (Boston: Little, Brown Co., 1978), pp. 54-61.
3. For analysis of the 1968 results, see Gerald Wright, *Electoral Choice in America* (Chapel Hill: Institute for Research in Social Science, 1974), pp. 59-64. The Senate responses for 1974 were computed by the author from data in the 1974 National Election Study. No open-ended questions have been asked for both the Senate and House in the same study or same election year.
4. The past comparative studies emphasize the differences between Senate and gubernatorial races. See Wright, *Electoral Choice,* and Barbara Hinckley et al., "Information and the Vote: A Comparative Election Study," *American Politics Quarterly* (April 1974): 131-158. These studies, of course, had not been able to compare the Senate and House results. While there are differences in state-wide voting for senator and governor, the differences between House and Senate voting appear even more substantial.
5. Donald Stokes and Warren Miller, "Party Government and the Salience of Congress," *Public Opinion Quarterly* (Winter 1962): 531-546.
6. Barbara Hinckley et al., "Information and the Vote," pp. 138, 139.
7. Ibid. Note that with only 13 state races included in the sample, a very salient issue in only one race might be observed in the overall results.
8. The variables are ranked by the size of their standardized regression coefficients. All variables cited in the text are significant at the .01 level. For the analysis, see Lyn Ragsdale, "The Fiction of Congressional Elections as Presidential Events," *American Politics Quarterly* (October 1980): 375-398. The analysis used ordinary least squares regression to determine the relative impact of the independent variables on an individual's partisan vote. A separate probit analysis was performed and replicated the regression results.
9. Richard Brody, "Communications," *American Political Science Review* (September 1976): 924. Brody also suggests use of the feeling thermometer measure.

10. As shown by Thomas Mann, *Unsafe At Any Margin* (Washington, D.C.: American Enterprise Institute, 1978), pp. 63-65.
11. Thomas Mann and Raymond Wolfinger, "Candidates and Parties in Congressional Elections," *American Political Science Review* (September 1980): 625.
12. Ibid.
13. *New York Times,* November 6, 1980, p. 17.
14. Robert Darcy and Sarah Schramm, "When Women Run Against Men," *Public Opinion Quarterly* (1977): 1-12.
15. Ibid., p. 10. Darcy and Schramm also suggest that the major restriction to the selection of women occurs at the point of recruitment and nominating processes.
16. Paul Dawson and James Zinser, "Characteristics of Campaign Resource Allocation in the 1972 Congressional Elections," in *Changing Campaign Techniques,* ed. L. Sandy Maisel, *Sage Electoral Studies Yearbook,* vol. 2 (Beverly Hills: Sage Publications, 1976), p. 93.

6

The Issues

There comes a time in every campaign speech or political gathering when the candidate must "discuss the issues." While members of Congress may specialize in one or two areas of their committee work, they are, nonetheless, expected to have opinions on all the major questions confronting the nation. Those listening to the candidates expect it; the news media search for it; and the candidates assume it themselves.

This expectation clearly accords with the traditional democratic theory of elections. Voters need to know the candidates' stands on issues in order to choose who should represent them in the government. But those people giving, writing, and reporting the speeches—as well as those attending them—may not reflect the attitudes and opinions of the wider electorate. We need to look beyond this surface attention to issues to determine their real importance in congressional voting.

Some preliminary clarification is in order. What, in fact, is an *issue?* What does this word mean that is used so frequently in both academic and popular political discussions? The dictionary definition helps only a little. An issue, according to *Webster's New Collegiate Dictionary,* is "a matter that is in dispute"; "a point of debate or controversy." Political issues are usually considered to involve questions of public policy. Thus people speak of economic issues, foreign policy issues, or other kinds of issues. But an issue is not synonymous with a *policy;* it is a point considered debatable about a policy. Neither is an issue merely any theme or point of policy subject to debate: many such subjects never become issues or become issues at one time and not at another. Issues, it appears, must be "raised": i.e., they must be brought to people's attention as worthy of discussion and debate. They may be raised by the candidates themselves, by interest groups, by the news media, or by others. Issues do not simply occur—they are created. We might consider the following definition as a guideline: *issues are questions of public policy held by some people to be controversial and worth debate and discussion.*

This definition clarifies the subject in a number of ways. First, note the qualification, "by some people." General agreement that a subject is controversial or worth debate is unnecessary. Indeed, a very small minority might consider a subject to be an issue and vote accordingly.[1] Second, nothing in the definition says that people must agree on what the question is or on the lines of debate. Issues may be deliberately blurred or differently defined. Third, these questions of public policy can be very general or specific. In election studies, a candidate's ideology is usually considered along with the more specific issue positions. Ideology is a general and integrated political belief system that helps shape more specific attitudes: for example, a conservative ideology might help shape attitudes toward defense, federal spending, and abortion. Defining questions of public policy broadly to include both very general and specific attitudes allows us to consider the effects of ideology with the more specific issue positions. Finally, limiting the definition to questions of public policy screens out the candidate qualifications discussed in the preceding chapter. It is true that often the candidates themselves, by their attributes or behavior, are the real issues in a campaign. Someone's age or sex or failure to report income is the issue. It is also true that many of these attributes or actions can have policy implications. By this definition, however, the candidate-related questions are treated separately. We can thus compare the relative importance of candidates and issues in an election.

Most of the writing about issue voting is silent on the subject of definitions. These guidelines, however, should be useful in the subsequent discussion. Candidates and parties are perceived to take various stands on issues: i.e., on questions of public policy held by some people to be controversial and worth debate and discussion. So we will ask about the importance of these stands—and the voters' perception of these stands—to the election result.

THE ISSUE VOTING CONTROVERSY

Questions about issue voting—its extent, substance, and measurement—have figured prominently in political science research. However, like so much of the voting behavior literature, the studies have focused on presidential elections. This literature can be used as a base for questions about congressional issue voting. The congressional research, in turn, should both clarify and expand the knowledge on the subject.

The traditional view of the informed issue-oriented voter was first challenged by evidence from survey research. In a study called *Voting* (1954), Bernard Berelson and his associates raised questions about the extent of the public's political information and interest.[2] Citizens, they found, knew little about labor legislation or price controls, issues that were highly visible and controversial in the 1948 presidential election. Even the voters who did know about these issues tended to misinterpret the presidential candidates' positions to make them accord with their own views. For instance, a voter who favored the pro-labor Taft-Hartley Act and supported Republican presidential candidate Thomas Dewey would see Dewey, incorrectly, as supporting Taft-Hartley and Harry S. Truman as opposing it. The election would decide which candidate's view of these policies would be brought to the White House, but the decision was based on little public information about the issues.

The challenge was intensified with the first major nationwide survey results reported in *The American Voter* (1960).[3] The study proposed three minimum conditions necessary for issue voting and examined what proportion of citizens across the nation could meet these conditions. People would have to be (1) aware of the issue, (2) concerned somewhat about the issue (have a position on it), and (3) perceive one party or candidate as closer to their own position than the other. Of course, people could meet these conditions and yet vote for reasons that had nothing to do with issues; therefore, the proportion fulfilling the three conditions represents an upper limit or maximum estimate of the potential for issue voting. The study reported that approximately one-fourth to one-third of the respondents could meet these minimum conditions for the major controversial issues of the 1950s. Examples from the 16 issues selected are shown below:

	Percentage of Respondents Aware of, Opinionated About, and Able to Place Candidate or Party on the Issues
Act tough toward Russia and China	36
Influence of big business in government	35
Influence of unions in government	31
Firing of suspected communists	23
Leave electricity and housing to private industry	22
Economic aid to foreign countries	23
Insure medical care	24

The authors of the study summarize the results:

It seems, then, that the sequence of events that must intervene before bitter partisan controversy dramatized in the press becomes significant for the political response of the man-in-the-street is both lengthy and fallible. Many people fail to appreciate that an issue exists, others are insufficiently involved to pay attention to recognized issues, and still others fail to make connections between issue positions and party policy.[4]

Other evidence from *The American Voter* was supplied by open-ended questions asking people what they liked and disliked about the two major political parties. Answers showing some issue awareness could be distinguished from those showing only party or candidate-oriented concerns. Two examples from the many cited in the study capture something of the flavor of the results.

Issue-Content:

(Like about Democrats?) I think the Democrats are more concerned with all the people. (How do you mean?) They put out more liberal legislation for all the people.

(Dislike about Democrats?) They have a sordid history over the past 20 years, though no worse than the Republican Administration. (How do you mean?) Oh, things like deep freezes and corruption in government.

(Like about Republicans?) No!

(Dislike about Republicans?) Oh, they're more for a moneyed group.

No Issue-Content; Candidate Response:

(Like about Democrats?) I haven't heard too much. I don't get any great likes or dislikes.

(Dislike about Democrats?) I hate the darned backbiting.

(Like about Republicans?) No.

(Dislike about Republicans?) No.

(Like about Stevenson?) No, I don't like him at all.

(Dislike about Stevenson?) I have no use for Stevenson whatsoever. I had enough of him at the last election. I don't like the cut-throat business—condemn another man and then shake hands with him five minutes later.

(Like about Eisenhower?) As a man I like Eisenhower better. Not particularly for the job of President, but he is not so apt to cut your throat.

(Dislike about Eisenhower?) No.

About one-fourth of the sample could be classified as having no issue content in the response.[5]

The thrust of the findings, and the point capturing readers' attention, was the low level of citizens' information about issues. However, it is important to note that the findings are mixed. Three-fourths of the people *did* show some issue awareness in their open-ended responses. One-fourth to one-third *could* be classified as potential issue voters. It is the old question of whether the glass of water is half empty or half full. Measured against the ideal of a citizenry fully informed and concerned about issues, the survey results reported in *The American Voter* appear shocking, but a careful reading of these results supports a view of an electorate where issues make a difference.

These early voting studies were challenged by a number of writers who argued that issues were important. Some pointed out that improved measurement techniques could show increased levels of issue voting. David RePass, for example, criticized the use of issues *preselected* by the researcher as important, contending that respondents should be asked to define the issues important to them. His results showed that more than 60 percent of the respondents could perceive differences between the parties on many of the issues they defined as important.[6] (The authors of *The American Voter* had found that between 40 and 60 percent of those having opinions on preselected issues could perceive party differences.) Other writers cautioned that it might not be the voters' fault that they could not perceive party differences if, in fact, the differences were blurred during the campaign by the candidates and parties themselves.[7] Still other writers pointed out that the 1950s might be a particularly unfortunate time to measure issue voting. People "liked Ike," supported the status quo, and showed little intense political involvement. In contrast, the more controversial years of the 1960s and 1970s might show stronger evidence for issue voting.

Richard Boyd conducted a normal vote analysis of the 1968 election and concluded that attitudes about Vietnam, race and urban unrest, and Lyndon Johnson's performance as president were all highly related to the vote.[8] Gerald Pomper examined the results of presidential-election-year surveys from 1956 to 1968 that included questions on six issues: school integration, medical care, fair employment practices, aid to education, a job guarantee, and foreign aid. He found that the percentage of people perceiving party differences on these issues did increase during this period. Of the four election years, the 1964 election represented the high point in awareness of party differences for all of the issues; the 1968 election was clearly higher than either the 1956 or the 1960 elections on three of the six issues (medical care, school integration, and fair employment) and slightly higher on one more (aid to education).[9] Since Barry Goldwater's presidential candidacy in 1964 claimed to offer voters "a choice and not an echo," it is important to note the higher perception of party differences in that election year.

Altogether, a very large literature has reasserted the importance of issues in voting behavior. People could discriminate between the candidates on the basis of issues. Elections could once again be seen, according to Gerald Pomper, as "meaningful democratic acts."[10]

In reviewing the issue voting controversy, two observations are important. First, *the controversy itself may be somewhat illusory.* The actual findings have changed less dramatically than the summary comments of the writers. Issues appeared important for a sizable minority of citizens in the early years and continued to be important in the later studies, although, according to the measures provided, they may be more important in some years than others. More work is needed, following Pomper, in comparing issue voting over time and, following Boyd, in measuring the effect of issues when long-term factors are controlled. Second, *the controversy lacks depth beyond the presidential level.* Clearly, we cannot generalize about issues in "American voting behavior" merely from the one most visible contest. It is Congress that decides many questions of public policy considered controversial and worth debate and discussion. Congress has passed legislation on medical care and fair employment practices. It has appropriated funds for education and foreign aid, or refused to appropriate such funds, often overriding presidential wishes in the process. If national issues are decided by both president and Congress, then an issue vote for one and a nonissue vote for the other cannot so easily be called a meaningful democratic act.

ISSUE VOTING IN CONGRESSIONAL ELECTIONS

Although the congressional research on issues has been preliminary and partial, two distinct kinds of findings have been identified: those showing the voters' generally low awareness of issues in congressional races; and those showing that under some circumstances issues appear to make a difference to the vote. These findings will be discussed separately and then considered in combination.

Information About Issues

One point should be clear from the preceding chapters. If one looks at the number of people aware and informed, then the importance of issue voting appears to be low. A 1972 analysis confirms this observation found across time and in a number of studies. People were asked if they had positions on some major issues in the 1972 campaigns and if they could identify the parties' and the candidates' positions. Those responding "don't know" for questions about Vietnam, welfare, and a general liberal-to-conservative ideological position are reported in Table 6-1. Respondents, it is clear, can place themselves on these issues and even identify their general ideological position. They are also quite able to place the parties and the presidential candidates: indeed, approximately 90 percent could do so for the Vietnam issue question. They are not able, however, to place the congressional candidates. More than half of the sample did not know their House candidate's position on any of the issues. More critically, knowing the position of the party (from 11 to 17 percent "don't knows") evidently did not help them define the position of the congressional candidate (from 56 to 60 percent "don't knows"). This is especially striking since the question supplied the name of the party and asked where one would place the Democratic or Republican candidate for Congress in the district. Partisans, in fact, reported as many "don't knows" about the congressional candidates as Independents.[11]

Interestingly, Vietnam and welfare were also the issues considered the most important problems facing the national government. When asked what the most important problems were, 46 percent gave a Vietnam or peace-related response and 19 percent a welfare-related response. In second responses, 8 and 24 percent respectively cited Vietnam and welfare. Note also that the position of the incumbent was available in 1972: roll-call votes on both Vietnam and welfare had occurred in the House in the preceding Congress. So, people could cite the most important issues, place themselves and the parties and presidential candidates on these issues, but they could not place the congressional candidates, even when their positions could be known.

Essentially the same pattern is shown for the 1978 results. (See Table 6-2.) People were asked to place the parties and candidates on the same liberal-to-conservative dimension and on a number of issues, including the government's role in ensuring jobs and an adequate standard of living and in helping minority groups. Most people could place Jimmy Carter and both the Democratic and Republican parties on these issues; fewer could place the Senate candidates, and fewer still the House candidates. Again, as in the 1972 study, the name of the candidate's party was supplied. Party may supply a low-information cue

Table 6-1 Information About Issues, 1972: Percentage of "Don't Know" Responses*

	Self	Party		Presidential Candidates		Congressional Candidates	
		D	R	D	R	D	R
Vietnam	4	12	11	10	9	59	60
Welfare	3	16	14	13	11	60	59
Liberalism-Conservatism	7	17	16	18	17	58	56

* Percentages are based on a Wisconsin state-wide sample (N=841) interviewed after the election of 1972. People giving "Don't Know" responses are those who could not place the people or the parties on the seven-point issue scales provided.

SOURCE: Barbara Hinckley, "Issues, Information Costs, and Congressional Elections," *American Politics Quarterly* (April 1976): 131-152. By permission of the Publisher, Sage Publications, Inc.

Table 6-2 Information About Issues, 1978: Percentage of "Don't Know" Responses*

	President	Party		Senate Candidates		House Candidates	
		D	R	D	R	D	R
Job Guarantee	13	18	20	37	36	53	60
Help for Minorities	12	21	24	45	45	56	65
Liberalism-Conservatism	10	15	15	34	35	50	57

* Percentages are based on those respondents who could place themselves on the issue and those (in the columns for Senate and House candidates) who were in districts or states where the Democratic or Republican candidates were running for election.

SOURCE: Compiled by the author from the 1978 National Election Study.

for making voting decisions, but it evidently does not help people assess the positions of congressional candidates.

As expected, one finds from the 1978 study that incumbents are rated on issues much more frequently than their opponents. Altogether, 20 percent of the "informed" respondents (those who could place themselves on the issues) could also place both House candidates. One has a measure of potential issue voting to compare with the earlier presidential results. The percentages of people rating both, only one, or no House candidates on issues are shown in Table 6-3.

Again, is the glass partly empty or partly full? By these results, only 20 percent of the sample (and somewhat more for the voters) would

Table 6-3 Information about Issues: Percentage Who Could Rate House Candidates (N=1803)

	Job Guarantee	Minority Help	Liberalism-Conservatism
Neither Candidate	52	52	53
One Candidate Only	29	27	26
Both Candidates	20	21	21

SOURCE: Sally Friedman, "The Role of Issues in Congressional Elections" (Paper presented at the annual meeting of the American Political Science Association, Washington, D.C., August 28-31, 1980), p. 27. Friedman points out that about 30 percent could place the two candidates on at least one issue across the series of issue questions.

fulfill the requirement of traditional democratic theory that citizens compare both candidates' positions with their own position in order to make a selection. At the same time, 20 percent is a sizable potential impact in an election. Sally Friedman reports that between 20 and 30 percent of those rating the candidates see their position to be in accord with their own positions: i.e., they rate themselves and the candidates at the same point on the seven-point issue scales. Between 50 and 60 percent place themselves no more than one unit apart on the seven-point scales. What one finds, Friedman argues, is "single-alternative" voting: people vote for the candidate known and seen as acceptable on issues.[12] Single-alternative voting can be understood in terms of the discussion in Chapter 1. Given limits on time and interest, voters who see one candidate as acceptable have no need to seek further information. Of course, issue agreement can be misperceived or affected by the perceptual screen of partisanship or the warm glow of incumbent popularity. Nevertheless, these single-alternative voters, like those who consider two alternatives, may make use of issues to help make their selection.

An additional finding is important. When we use open-ended rather than preselected questions, we find no increased issue awareness among the citizens. This alternative measure, proposed in the issue voting controversy, does not improve the analysis of congressional results. For example, people in 1978 were asked what was "the most important single issue" in the House campaign in their district. Only one-third of the national sample could cite an issue in response; and of those, less than one-half preferred a candidate because of the issue: that is to say, only 13 percent of the full sample preferred a candidate because of an issue in the campaign. (All responses to the question are included, no matter what people called a campaign issue.) In the races between incumbents and challengers, incumbents were preferred on the issues 78 percent of the time. Since this is about the same preference rate for incumbents in the full sample, independently of any issues, the campaign issues do not appear to be significantly changing the results. People were also asked what they thought was the most important problem facing the country and whether there would be differences between the parties and candidates in dealing with this problem. In Table 6-4 the contrast in the percentages able to answer the question parallels the results seen earlier for the preselected issue questions.

People can name what they think are the most important problems, judge the job "the government" is doing handling these problems, and say whether one party or the other would do a better job, or whether there would be no difference between them. They see Congress as having more say than the president. But they cannot judge the job the House candidates would do on these problems. (Note that those perceiving no difference between the parties or candidates are counted as giving an

Table 6-4   Most Important Problem Facing the Country

	(N)	Percentage "Don't Know"[1]
Cite most important problem facing the country	(2304)	5
Judge job the government is doing in dealing with the problem	(2304)	8
Say whether there are differences between the parties on these problems	(2304)	13
Say whether there are differences between the House candidates on these problems	(1841)[2]	62

Importance of Congress and the President in What Government Does[3]	(N)	Percentage
Congress more important	(2304)	51
Both equal	(2304)	33
President more important	(2304)	12
Don't Know; No Answer	(2304)	4

[1] Includes those who cannot answer the question and those who cannot cite a most important problem facing the country.

[2] Includes only those respondents in districts with a contest between two major party candidates.

[3] The question asked, "In general, thinking of the most important problems facing the country, which do you think has the most say in what our government does—the Congress, the President, or are they about equal?"

SOURCE: Compiled by the author from the 1978 National Election Study.

answer and not as a "Don't Know" response.) The problems are important and Congress is important, but these perceptions are not connected with the positions of the candidates for Congress.

The importance attributed to Congress reinforces earlier findings and deserves emphasis. People's low issue awareness of House candidates apparently does not stem from a low regard for Congress as an institution.[13] The perception of the institution appears not to be connected with the perception of its individual members. People can dislike Congress but like their own representative.[14] They hold Congress—not the incumbent—responsible for government problems. To some extent, this disjunction is encouraged by the members themselves:

it is clearly to the advantage of incumbents not to be held accountable for the perceived failings of government. To some extent, too, it may be built in from the collective nature of the institution. Unlike governors or presidents or other executives, a member of Congress is only one of 535 House and Senate members. The result, in any case, is a situation where the issues debated in Congress are not considered by the voters in selecting congressional candidates.

Issues and the Vote

There is a second set of findings, however, that needs to be considered. While the voters' general awareness of issues may be low, under some circumstances the candidates' stands on the issues and citizen perceptions of these stands can make a difference to the vote. The evidence, while not overwhelming, comes from both aggregate and survey results.

How does the members' behavior in Congress affect the voting results? Robert Erikson finds that House members taking relatively extreme positions on roll-call votes in Congress, compared to other party members, do less well at the polls than the more moderate members even when district differences are controlled for. The effect is clearest for conservative Republicans compared to other Republicans, and somewhat less clear for liberal Democrats.[15] Similar findings are seen in 1964—when Republican representatives endorsing Barry Goldwater for president fared less well electorally than did those not endorsing him[16]—and in 1974, when electoral losses appeared largest among the most conservative Republicans in the House.[17]

Few issues facing Congress have been as keenly watched and widely visible as the impeachment question faced by members of the House Judiciary Committee in the spring and summer of 1974. Here, if anywhere, through the long days of nationwide television coverage, we might expect that information on issues was communicated to voters. A study conducted by Gerald Wright examined the electoral impact of the committee members' pro- and anti-impeachment stands. Wright constructed an expected baseline vote, using party voting and incumbency, and measured the deviation from that baseline in the actual vote received. The short-term effect of the impeachment stand could thus be measured against the long-term effects of party and incumbency. He found that Republicans voting for impeachment (and against Nixon) averaged five percentage points better than expected and that Republicans voting against impeachment did worse than expected. No clear differences, however, were found for the Democrats on the Judiciary Committee.[18]

All of these studies, it is interesting to note, find evidence that supports issue voting for the Republicans and not the Democrats. Why this should be so is a puzzle that needs further investigation.

Similar moderate effects are seen in the survey results. By a variety of measures, issues can be shown to be significantly related to the vote when the effects of party identification and incumbency are not controlled. However, we know from the preceding chapters that these two factors themselves affect both issue perceptions and the vote. Few attempts have been made to measure the electoral effect of issues independently of party and incumbency. One study finds for 1966 that party defection increases as voters move closer to the issue position of the opposing party's candidate and that the greater the distance between candidates on issues, the more likely such defection.[19] Analysis of the open-ended questions for 1978 shows that references to issues remain significantly related to the vote independently of the effects of party and incumbency.[20]

How can issues affect the vote, given the generally low issue-awareness of congressional voters? One explanation was suggested earlier: small numbers of voters can make a difference in an election. These marginal effects can be seen when party and incumbency are controlled. However, we still need to confront the fact that issue perceptions are highly correlated with party identification and support for incumbents. It appears that additional information brings an increased *interconnection* among the various attitude components through which one's perception of issues comes to support one's attitudes toward the parties and the incumbent. One finds a convergence of thinking. Some evidence of this effect is seen for both presidential and congressional voters. As information increases—from the congressional to the presidential race and from less to more attentive voters—one finds higher correlations between issue and party positions.[21] Issue perceptions, then, may work more to strengthen and elaborate existing attitudes than to produce independent effects.

Indirect Effects

The candidates' stands on issues may have effects untapped by these aggregate and survey measures. In contrast to the general public, some groups of people are very aware of the candidates' positions on issues and are willing to raise and spend money to bring the winner's position more in line with their own position. Some interest groups are concerned about single issues, high in controversy and prominent on the congressional agenda: gun control, abortion, labor legislation, regulation of small or large businesses. Thus the Gun Owners of America will work to elect or defeat candidates who support or oppose their positions on gun control. Other groups—the conservative National Conservative Political Action Committee (NCPAC) or the liberal National Committee for an Effective Congress (NCEC) for example—are more broadly ideological, targeting conservative or liberal candidates expected to vote "right" (or "wrong") on a wide range of legislation before the Congress.

According to the results in Chapter 2, campaign spending helps candidates, and especially challengers, in getting across a minimum threshold of voter awareness in a campaign. Therefore, the specific positions and general ideology of candidates can create indirect effects by provoking spending (for or against a candidate), which in turn affects visibility and the vote. For instance, voters may be generally unaware of the liberalism and conservatism of two House candidates in a race, but the reason that there *is* a race—and a hotly contested one—is that some groups are supporting the challenger or opposing the incumbent. Indeed, the impact of issues in congressional elections may be seriously underestimated if we ignore these indirect effects.

Measurement difficulties can help explain why such effects have not been studied more seriously. Few groups will publish their "enemies list" of candidates targeted for defeat. Since campaign literature and journalistic accounts often disagree as to who and how many are being targeted, one has no easily available or systematic measure for the inputs against which to measure the voting results. One has only ad hoc accounts and examples that may or may not be representative of a larger pattern of effects. Nevertheless, the available accounts are intriguing and suggest the value of more systematic study.

Table 6-5 shows some candidates in the 1978 Senate and House elections that were supported or opposed by conservative groups. Two Democratic liberal Senate incumbents, among possible others, were targeted for defeat: Dick Clark of Iowa and Thomas McIntyre of New Hampshire. Both lost, although very narrowly. At the same time, two conservative Republican incumbents—Jesse Helms of North Carolina and Strom Thurmond of South Carolina—were supported with large fund-raising efforts against strong challengers supported by liberal groups. Both Helms and Thurmond were re-elected. In a fifth Senate race, for an open seat in New Jersey, the conservative-supported candidate was defeated. In the House, the conservative efforts were less successful. Of the five incumbents targeted for defeat, four were re-elected.[22]

In 1980, conservative groups targeted at least six liberal Democratic senators for defeat and succeeded in unseating four: George McGovern of South Dakota, Birch Bayh of Indiana, John Culver of Iowa, and Frank Church of Idaho.[23] The senators' opponents would all be considered within the more conservative faction of the Republican party. In particular, Indiana's Dan Quayle had developed a reputation as a strong conservative in the House, was supported by conservative groups, and received approximately one-quarter of his $750,000 in contributions from business-related political action committees.[24] Iowa's Charles Grassley

Table 6-5   Selected Senate and House Candidates Supported or Opposed by Conservatives, with 1978 Election Results

Supported Candidates	Opposed Candidates	Result Winner	Vote Margin (% Total Vote)
Senate			
Roger Jepsen (R-Iowa)	Dick Clark (D)	Jepsen†	52
Gordon Humphrey (R-N.H.)	Thomas McIntyre (D)	Humphrey†	51
Jeffrey Bell (R-N.J.)	Bill Bradley (D)	Bradley	56
Jesse Helms (R-N.C.)	John Ingram (D)	Helms†	54
Strom Thurmond (R-S.C.)	Charles Ravenel (D)	Thurmond†	56
House			
Ron Paul (R-Tex.)	Bob Gammage (D)	Paul†	50
John Cunningham (R-Wash.)	Mike Lowry (D)	Lowry	54
Ed Scott (R-Colo.)	Timothy Wirth (D)	Wirth	53
John Porter (R-Ill.)	Abner Mikva (D)	Mikva	50
Saul Harris (R-Md.)	Gladys Spellman (D)	Spellman	78
Mike Conlin (R-Mich.)	Bob Carr (D)	Carr	58

NOTE: The names of incumbents are italicized. A dagger (†) designates that the conservative candidate won. For details, see *Electing Congress* (Washington, D.C.: Congressional Quarterly, 1978) pp. 22, 23; and *Congressional Quarterly Weekly Report*, November 11, 1978, pp. 3244-3247, 3262.

was seen as a strong conservative and supported by New Right and religious fundamentalist groups opposing abortion, gun control, and the equal rights amendment.[25] Of the six liberal senators, all but Eagleton were defeated. But it is not known to what extent these group efforts were a factor in the results or, indeed, how a group's success or failure might be measured. These examples suggest the kinds of questions that need pursuing. How can a universe of such targeted races be determined, and how can group influence be systematically measured? Is a 54 percent victory for incumbent Helms or a 51 percent victory for challenger Humphrey "low" or "high" when calculated against the expected vote from party and incumbency?

Much of the issue voting research has attempted to show that candidates' positions make a difference at the polls and that issues are important in American elections. A study of these indirect effects is one way that research might be continued.

SUMMARY

The importance of issues in American voting can be clarified by the congressional results. Beyond the presidential contest, information about issues drops sharply: approximately one-half of the citizens could place neither of the House candidates on the issues and about 20 percent could place both candidates. There are no signs, on the surface at least, that congressional information has increased over the years; nor has the use of open-ended rather than preselected questions improved results. While we find evidence that the issues that are perceived affect the vote, both the perceptions and the vote are closely interconnected with attitudes about parties and the incumbent. Much more work is needed measuring the short-term effects of issues beyond party and incumbency and measuring indirect effects. Since the candidates' positions on issues are very important to some people, we need a more systematic study of how this importance can affect the election results.

The issue voting controversy appears to have exaggerated the differences in the findings of the various studies; hence, we need caution in adding the congressional results. No one is arguing—for presidential or congressional races—that all citizens make choices on the basis of issues. Moreover, no one is denying that a potentially important minority of citizens may be issue voters. At the presidential level, some portion of citizens—and the estimates range from 40 to 60 percent— fulfill the minimum conditions for issue voting. But these people do not necessarily use issues in their voting or use them against their party identification. At the congressional level, some portion of citizens also fulfills the minimum conditions for issue voting, and here the estimates range closer to 20 or 30 percent. But these people also do not necessarily use issues in their vote or against their party's candidates. Eliminating the extremes of interpretation should be helpful in focusing attention on the very real questions of issue voting that remain.

NOTES

1. Presumably, at the extreme, an individual could consider a subject controversial and worth debate when no one else did, seek differences between the candidates or parties, and vote accordingly. Most people would probably want to call that individual an issue voter.
2. Bernard Berelson, Paul Lazarsfeld, and William McPhee, *Voting* (Chicago: University of Chicago Press, 1954).
3. Angus Campbell et al., *The American Voter* (New York: John Wiley & Sons, 1960), p. 180.
4. Ibid., p. 183.
5. Ibid., p. 246. For example cited, see pp. 232, 348. See also Philip Converse, "The Nature of Belief Systems in Mass Publics," in *Ideology and Discontent*, ed. David Apter (New York: The Free Press, 1964), pp. 206-261.
6. David RePass, "Issue Salience and Party Choice," *American Political Science Review* (June 1971): 389-400.
7. Richard Brody and Benjamin Page, "Policy Voting and the Electoral Process: The Vietnam War Issue," *American Political Science Review* (September 1972): 979-995.
8. Richard Boyd, "Popular Control of Public Policy: A Normal Vote Analysis of the 1968 Election," *American Political Science Review* (June 1972): 424-449.
9. Gerald Pomper, "From Confusion to Clarity: Issues and American Voters, 1956-1968," *American Political Science Review* (June 1972): 415-428. See also Norman Nie and Kristi Andersen, "Mass Belief Systems Revisited," *Journal of Politics* (August 1974): 540-587. For an important critique of Pomper and of other accounts of increased issue voting, see Michael Margolis, "From Confusion to Confusion: Issues and the American Voter (1956-1972)," *American Political Science Review* (March 1977): 31-43.
10. Gerald Pomper, "Rejoinder," *American Political Science Review* (June 1972): 466. See John Kessel, "The Issues in Issue Voting," *American Political Science Review* (June 1972): 459-465. Kessel counts some 30 books, articles, and convention papers written by 1972 on the importance of issues in presidential voting.
11. Barbara Hinckley, "Issues, Information Costs, and Congressional Elections," *American Politics Quarterly* (April 1976): 131-152.
12. Sally Friedman, "The Role of Issues in Congressional Elections" (Paper presented at the annual meeting of the American Political Science Association, Washington, D.C., August 28-31, 1980), p. 17.
13. See Hinckley, "Issues, Information Costs, and Congressional Elections."
14. Richard Fenno, "If, As Ralph Nader Says, Congress is 'The Broken Branch,' How Come We Love Our Congressmen So Much?" in *Congress in Change*, ed. Norman Ornstein (New York: Praeger Publishers, 1975), pp. 277-287.
15. Robert Erikson, "The Electoral Impact of Congressional Roll Call Voting," *American Political Science Review* (December 1971): 1018-1032.
16. Robert Schoenberger, "Campaign Strategy and Party Loyalty," *American Political Science Review* (June 1969): 515-520.

17. Walter Dean Burnham, "Insulation and Responsiveness in Congressional Elections," *Political Science Quarterly* (Fall 1975): 411-436.

18. Gerald Wright, "Constituency Response to Congressional Behavior: The Impact of the House Judiciary Committee Impeachment Votes," *Western Political Quarterly* (September 1977): 401-410. Wright also tests the impact of general ideological conservatism, but finds that this cannot explain the results.

19. Gerald Wright, "Candidates' Policy Positions and Voting in U.S. Congressional Elections," *Legislative Studies Quarterly* (August 1976): 445-464.

20. See Glenn Parker, "Incumbent Popularity and Electoral Success," *Sage Electoral Studies Yearbook,* vol. 6, ed. L. Sandy Maisel and Joseph Cooper (Beverly Hills: Sage Publications, 1981); and Lyn Ragsdale, "The Fiction of Congressional Elections as Presidential Events," *American Politics Quarterly* (October 1980): 375-398. See also M. Margaret Conway and Mikel Wyckoff, "Voter Choice in the 1974 Congressional Elections," *American Politics Quarterly* (January 1980): 3-14. Conway and Wyckoff find that issues show relatively little impact on the vote beyond the effects of party, incumbency, and the candidate's visibility.

21. Hinckley, "Issues, Information Costs, and Congressional Elections," pp. 140-143.

22. The races cited are those identified by Congressional Quarterly in *Electing Congress* (Washington, D.C.: Congressional Quarterly, 1978), pp. 22, 23 and in *Congressional Quarterly Weekly Report,* November 11, 1978, pp. 3244-3247, 3262.

23. See *Congressional Quarterly Weekly Report,* October 11, 1980, p. 2984. The names cited as the liberals targeted for defeat will vary slightly depending on the source reporting.

24. Ibid., pp. 3011, 3012.

25. Ibid., pp. 3015.

7

The Curious Case of the
Midterm Election

One puzzle of American elections that has intrigued generations of political observers is the congressional midterm election result. In every twentieth-century midterm election but one—1934—the president's party has lost seats in the House. While some loss of seats has become a predictable occurrence, the size of the loss has varied widely—recently ranging as large as 48 seats and as small as 5 seats. The midterm election is the off-year election, with no presidential race. So why should the president's party lose seats? Why should the loss be so consistent? And what can explain the size of the variation?

These three questions have importance for interpreting any particular election result. Was the 16-seat loss for the Democrats in 1978 a bad thing—since it was a loss—or a good thing—since many midterm losses have been larger? In 1970, at the height of the Vietnam war controversy, the Republicans lost 12 seats. The Nixon White House argued that this loss was a show of support for the administration and its policies since it was well below average for a midterm year. But what is an average, or an expected loss, and how can it be measured? We need to understand the phenomenon before we know what to measure any one case against. The questions have particular importance for their presidential implications. The midterm results are considered in popular political commentary to be a verdict on the presidential administration. Voters are given the chance to tell presidents how they are doing halfway through their term. The election results, then, become a kind of vote of confidence or no confidence in the American executive. Richard Nixon is told something by the 12-seat loss in 1970, Jimmy Carter by the 16-seat loss in 1978, or Lyndon Johnson by the 48-seat loss in 1966. Remember, however, that the voters are voting for *House* candidates. We cannot be sure that they are "saying" something about the president or what, if anything, is being said.

The midterm results, therefore, have even broader implications for understanding congressional elections. They concern the president as an influence on congressional voting. So beyond the influences of party, incumbency, candidates, and issues, we need to examine if there are other, presidential effects. If we accept the notion of a midterm verdict, we have to assume some link between the voter's perception of the presidential administration and the voter's perception of the congressional candidate's party. Is there, indeed, such a link, and if so, how does it affect the congressional vote?

With a puzzle so intriguing and important, it is not surprising that many writers have attempted to unravel it. In the past, two main explanations have been offered: one concentrates on presidential coattails and a changing electorate between the presidential-year and the off-year elections; the other looks to the negative voting against the president or the president's party in the off-year election. This chapter will examine the insights and shortcomings of both explanations and will then advance a somewhat broader, although tentative, explanation.

PRESIDENTIAL COATTAILS AND THE TWO ELECTORATES

Explanation

One explanation has focused on the coattails or "pulling power" of the presidential vote. Candidates are said to have coattails when their own electoral popularity helps other candidates win election who would not have won otherwise. In terms of the metaphor, candidates ride into office on the more popular candidate's coattails. Historically, presidential coattails have been observed in congressional elections. As the vote for one party's presidential candidate increases state by state or district by district, the vote for that party's congressional candidate also increases. In other words, the greater the vote for a party's presidential candidate, the less likely is defeat for its congressional candidates. This effect, it should be noted, is separate from partisanship. Even after controlling for party, we can see across a number of years of American elections that as the vote for the presidential candidate of one party increases, the vote for congressional candidates of the same party also increases.[1] Something, beyond party identification, appears to be helping the congressional candidates of the same party as the president win elections in presidential-election years.

So in the midterm election, without the president on the ticket, the seats are lost that would otherwise have been lost before. Much of the loss for the president's party at the midterm may be simply a loss built in by the victory two years earlier. The more House candidates carried to victory on presidential coattails, the more House seats that may be lost in the midterm election when the coattails are not there to hang on to. In short, the amount of midterm loss may be directly related to the amount of presidential popularity in the preceding election. By this argument, the Democratic party's loss of 48 seats in 1966 said less about Johnson in 1966 than it did about his popularity in the landslide election of 1964, when the Democrats gained 37 seats. The Republican party's loss of 12 seats in 1970 said less about the Nixon administration at the time than it did about the Republicans' inability to gain seats in 1968, when they won only a net of five.

A second part of the explanation points to the two different electorates voting for Congress in the presidential year and the off year. (Recall the marked disparity between presidential and off-year voter turnout shown in Figure 2-1.) As Angus Campbell argues, a midterm election brings the habitual, more interested, and more partisan voter to the polls, whereas the presidential election attracts both habitual and marginal voters, the latter attracted by the excitement of the presidential contest. According to Campbell, in any presidential election one or the other candidate has an advantage of party, personality, or some salient issue that attracts the less politically interested voters, as well as some habitual voters. But in the off year, that small proportion of habitual voters who defected returns to the party fold, and most importantly, the less interested portion of the electorate stays home. Both events hurt the party whose presidential and House candidates had the advantage in the previous election.[2]

According to this explanation, little is happening in the midterm election except for a sharp drop in turnout. There is an electoral surge and decline. The habitual voters continue to vote largely as before, despite some earlier defections, but the marginal voters—swinging to the president's party two years before—do not vote. The result of that 20 percentage point drop in turnout is that some candidates fall off the coattails they were riding.

Critique

This coattail explanation, however, is no longer widely accepted by political scientists. Three points of criticism are raised. First, coattails in presidential elections are not as apparent as they once were. With House members increasingly safe in their re-election, a presidential election brings in fewer coattail riders than before.[3] Incumbency counters the coattail effect. If coattails appear to be declining as an electoral force, then they cannot explain the continuing midterm loss of seats. Second, questions have been raised about the electoral surge and decline. Robert Arseneau and Raymond Wolfinger point out that the surge and decline thesis assumes there are two essentially different electorates in the presidential year and off year—the second more partisan, more educated, and more interested in politics than the first. However, when they examine survey results from three elections—1966 through 1970—they find little difference between presidential-year and off-year voters. The off-year voters in 1966 and 1970 are not noticeably more partisan, more educated, or more politically interested than the presidential-year voters in 1968.[4] In short, while more voters vote for House candidates in one election than the other, there is no reason to suppose that they vote differently. Third, more may be happening in the midterm election than the coattail argument would indicate, as the following section points out.

NEGATIVE VOTING IN THE MIDTERM ELECTION

Explanation

The second explanation interprets the midterm loss directly as a sign of voter disapproval with the presidential administration and the policies of government. There is "negative voting," Samuel Kernell argues, even though "the central figure—the President—is not on the ballot." He continues:

> Unlike presidential elections, the President is the only highly visible national actor in public view. Given poorly identified congressional contenders in many districts and no national counterpart from the other party, the president becomes the most prominent reference for choosing between candidates.[5]

Kernell cites three kinds of evidence in support of the negative voting thesis. First, Independents who disapprove of the president's performance are more likely to vote at the midterm than Independents who approve. Second, partisans who disapprove of their own party's president are more likely to defect from party lines in their congressional voting than are the partisans who approve. And third, the rates of defection are higher for the disapprovers within the president's party than among the approvers within the opposite party. In other words, negative presidential voting is a stronger force than positive presidential voting in explaining party defections in the congressional vote.

Economic policies in particular, some writers contend, may provoke voter dissatisfaction with presidents and the party in the White House. Evaluating general economic conditions or their own personal economic situation, voters may judge the party in the White House negatively and by transference the party of the congressional candidates. Accordingly, Edward Tufte explains the varying size of the midterm loss as a result of two factors: the president's general popularity as measured by Gallup polls; and economic well-being as measured by real disposable personal income. Tufte uses aggregate-level data for eight midterm elections and finds that the magnitude of the loss can be explained by these two factors. Like Kernell, he cites the lack of information available about congressional candidates and looks to the presidency for a cue for congressional voters. The midterm election, then, says more about the presidency than Congress. Tufte concludes, "The midterm is neither a mystery nor an automatic swing of the pendulum; the midterm vote is a referendum."[6] It is a presidential referendum.

This argument is part of a very large enterprise currently investigating the impact of economic factors on the vote. At the aggregate level, a number of studies have found a relationship between economic well-being and electoral support for the party in the White House. In relatively good times, the president's party is supported; in bad times, the opposing party is supported. The relationship holds using a variety of aggregate measures and for both presidential and congressional voting.[7] Presidential popularity itself is affected by changes in economic conditions.[8] However, studies at the individual level, using survey responses, find less support for the relationship. Perceptions of personal economic well-being do not appear related to the vote. People do not vote their own pocketbooks. They appear at times to judge the economy generally and the ability of the political parties to manage the economy, although even these judgments are not overwhelming in their influence.[9] Another study finds evidence for economic voting in presidential elections but not in congressional midterm elections.[10] On balance, then, while economic issues may affect the vote, through people's general evaluations of the state of the economy, they do not appear to constitute a major explanation of midterm election results.

The main components of the negative voting explanation can be identified as follows: (1) arguments for voters' low information about congressional candidates; (2) evidence from the Arseneau-Wolfinger study questioning the difference between presidential-year and off-year electorates; (3) evidence of increased voting for congressional candidates of the party opposing the president by voters who disapprove of the president's performance; and (4) aggregate-level evidence for the impact of presidential popularity and economic indicators on the congressional vote. Presidents are looked to as an "issue" in the midterm congressional campaigns since congressional-candidate voting (component 1) and an automatic adjustment from the presidential election (component 2) are eliminated as influences.

Critique

The evidence for negative voting, however, remains highly speculative. The Kernell study shows us that partisan disapprovers are more likely to defect from party in congressional voting than the approvers are. The main evidence for this proposition is reproduced in Table 7-1. Note first that most of the differences in defection rates between approvers and disapprovers are not statistically significant: in other words, the differences cannot be distinguished from a chance occurrence at .05 confidence levels. It is true that the differences are in the predicted direction; but given the lack of statistically significant findings, it would be at least as easy to *reject* the hypothesis that presidential approval or disapproval makes a difference to the congressional vote. Second and perhaps more critically, note that the possible effects of the strength of partisanship are not controlled for. We know that party identification affects the vote and also affects one's perception and evaluation of candidates. Strong Republicans and Democrats would be more likely than weak partisans (a) to vote for the party's congressional candidates and (b) to approve their own party's president or disapprove the opposing party's president. Hence some of the findings shown in Table 7-1 may be merely the result of partisan strength.

This indeed appears to be the case, as suggested by another study. James Piereson examines the relationship between presidential popularity and congressional voting for five categories of partisanship: strong and weak Democrats, strong and weak Republicans, and Independents (including those leaning toward the Democratic and Republican parties). He finds no tendency within the partisan groups for congressional voting to change with changes in presidential popularity; Independents, however, do show changes.[11] However, since Piereson combines Independent leaners with pure Independents, this combination may also be masking some partisan effects. In fact, when the Independents are separated, we find that little relationship remains between presidential popularity and congressional voting. Table 7-2 shows these results.

The table subdivides Kernell's dichotomous classification (same party of the president or other party) into the traditional seven-part identification scale. Only two groups of voters remain to support the negative voting thesis—weak Republicans and weak Democrats in 1974. Weak Republicans approving of the Republican president in 1974, Gerald R. Ford, were more likely to support Republican House candidates than those disapproving of the president; and weak Democrats approving of the Republican president were more likely to defect from their party and support Republican House candidates than those disapproving of the president. For the rest of the 1974 and 1978 voters, including Independents, approving or disapproving of the president made no difference to the congressional vote.

Another question is also worth raising. Evidence against the notion of the "two electorates" is cited as a reason for seeking alternative explanations. And yet that evidence, too, is highly speculative. The

Table 7-1 Presidential Popularity and Partisan Defections, 1946-1966

| | | Percentage Voting for Own Party's Congressional Candidate | | | | | |
| | | Election Year | | | | | |
Party Identification	Presidential Popularity	1946 (N) %	1950 (N) %	1954 (N) %	1958 (N) %	1962 (N) %	1966 (N) %
President's Party	Approve	(284) 89	(92) 96	(225) 96	(219) 93	(950) 90	(463) 92
	Disapprove	(218) 78	(164) 79	(8) —	(24) 81	(13) 62	(123) 78
	Difference	11%	17*%	—	12%	28%	14*%
Other Party	Approve	(165) 90	(40) 93	(92) 89	(119) 89	(370) 91	(155) 90
	Disapprove	(603) 98	(243) 98	(126) 97	(138) 96	(238) 98	(341) 97
	Difference	8*%	5%	8%	7%	7*%	7%

* Percentage point differences significant at .05.

SOURCE: Samuel Kernell, "Presidential Popularity and Negative Voting," *American Political Science Review* (March 1977): 58, table 5. The table excludes respondents in the South. © 1977 by American Political Science Association. Reprinted by permission.

Table 7-2   Presidential Popularity and Voting by Categories of Party Identification

Party Identification	Presidential Popularity	Republican President 1974 (N)	%	Democratic President 1978 (N)	%
	Percentage Voting for Own Party's Congressional Candidate				
Strong D	Approve	(55)	91	(52)	88
	Disapprove	(99)	91	(31)	84
Weak D	Approve	(68)	74	(147)	80
	Disapprove	(56)*	91	(48)	75
Independent D	Approve	(28)	84	(83)	61
	Disapprove	(49)	90	(32)	62
Independent R	Approve	(55)	60	(46)	61
	Disapprove	(10)	60	(55)	66
Weak R	Approve	(76)	74	(42)	62
	Disapprove	(33)*	55	(85)	68
Strong R	Approve	(76)	90	(30)	80
	Disapprove	(15)	87	(73)	79
	Percentage Voting for Congressional Candidate of the President's Party				
Independent Ind.	Approve	(30)	37	(61)	61
	Disapprove	(24)	50	(21)	48

* Percentage point differences significant at .05.

SOURCE: Supplied by Gary Mucciarone, Ph.D. candidate, University of Wisconsin, from a study of midterm congressional voting.

main analysis of the Arseneau-Wolfinger study is based on three elections only—two midterms and one presidential year. No tests of significance are conducted to see if there are, indeed, different voters in presidential years and off years. We do know from their study that approximately the same proportion of Independents vote in presidential years and off years and that the overall defection rate does not vary between the two kinds of elections. These figures, reproduced in Table 7-3, constitute the evidence at present against the two-electorate thesis.

As Table 7-3 makes clear, the percent of Independents voting does not vary systematically between presidential years and off years: i.e., 9 or 10 percent of the voters were Independents in the presidential-election years of 1972 and 1976 and in the off-year elections of 1974 and 1978. The defection rates, or the percentage of those who voted for House candidates of the opposite party, also do not vary systematically between the two kinds of elections. The defections increase over time, given the increasing tendency to vote for incumbents,[12] but they do not increase in presidential years and decrease in off years as the two-electorate thesis might lead one to expect. The off-year electorate is not necessarily more partisan than the presidential-year electorate.

These facts, however, are all we know. We do not know about possible differences in the two electorates in general political interest or in levels of information and interest concerning the congressional candidates. Nor do we know the defection rates for partisans of the president's party. The Arseneau-Wolfinger data in Table 7-3 combine both Republican and Democratic identifiers, whereas only one party might be affected in a given election year. The original argument proposed that there might be influences in any one presidential year favoring one party more than the other, such as pro-Democratic influences in 1964 or pro-Republican influences in 1980. For example, if Democrats, disaffected with Jimmy Carter in 1980, were less likely to vote than Republicans, such a turnout difference could hurt Democratic congressional candidates. Those Democratic voters, returning in 1982, would accordingly return some lost Democratic seats to the party. This argument cannot be tested without distinguishing both turnout and defection by party. Survey data from the 1950s to the present now exist to answer these questions.

Negative voting may occur, of course, with the same or a different electorate in the midterm: the two explanations are not necessarily contradictory. Nevertheless, more extensive testing of the two-electorate

Table 7-3 Vote for House Candidates by Party Identification, 1956-1978 (In Percentages)

	1956	58	60	62	64	66	68	70	72	74	76	78
For Own Party's Candidate	82	84	90	83	79	76	74	76	73	74	72	67
Against Own Party's Candidate	9	11	12	12	15	16	19	16	17	18	19	23
By Independents	9	5	8	6	5	8	7	8	10	9	9	10

SOURCE: Adapted from Robert Arseneau and Raymond Wolfinger, "Voting Behavior in Congressional Elections" (Paper presented at the annual meeting of the American Political Science Association, New Orleans, Louisiana, September 4-8, 1973), table 5. This data has been updated by Thomas Mann and Raymond Wolfinger in "Candidates and Parties in Congressional Elections," *American Political Science Review* (September 1980): 617-632.

thesis will be necessary before we can dismiss the coattail phenomenon or attempt any full explanation of the midterm election.

Finally, the negative voting studies may assume too easily that congressional factors are not important in congressional races. Incumbency, candidate evaluations, the effects of congressional issues are ignored. Presumably, we need to understand the impact of these factors before we can look to presidential or any other effects. One study provides some important evidence on the point. Lyn Ragsdale examines the relative and simultaneous effects of presidential popularity, incumbency, party identification, and congressional candidate evaluations.[13] Her results indicate that presidential popularity is a relatively weak predictor of the vote when the congressional factors are included in the analysis. While the presidential impact appears slightly greater in 1970 and 1974 than in 1978, in all of these years the nonpresidential variables are the major predictors of the vote, and congressional candidate evaluations are more important than presidential evaluations.

The influences on the congressional vote in the Ragsdale study are listed below in descending order of importance.[14] Presidential evaluations in the House were not found significantly related to the vote at the .01 confidence level. All other variables were significant at that level.

Senate 1974	*House 1978*
Party Identification	Candidate Personal Qualities
Candidate Experience	Party Identification
Candidate Personal Qualities	Incumbency
Candidate Issue Positions	Candidate Experience
Candidate Party Ties	Candidate Issue Positions
Incumbency	Candidate Party Ties
Presidential Evaluations	Presidential Evaluations

Presidential evaluations may not work directly, but indirectly through the perception of party ties with congressional candidates. Negative economic voting might work the same way, with people voting against the congressional candidate of the party in the White House. The results suggest, however, that party ties themselves are relatively unimportant, particularly in the House, compared to other candidate evaluations, party identification, and incumbency.

There are great difficulties, of course, in translating results from aggregate to individual levels or back again. Economic voting has been observed in the aggregate and not found important at the individual level, and the same may hold for presidential and party perceptions. There may be limits on the kind of survey question asked; the particular way that presidents or presidential parties are connected with congressional voting is difficult to tap in the survey responses. Further work is indicated, but the first results suggest that the president is not central to the congressional voting decision. Congressional influences—incumbency, candidate evaluations, and even the candidates' stands on issues—appear more important to the voting choice.

MEASURING SHORT-TERM EFFECTS

Despite their many differences, the coattail and negative voting explanations have important points in common. Both are speaking about short-term factors in congressional elections and both hypothesize that the president will have an effect: in the coattail argument, positively in presidential-year elections; and in the negative voting argument, negatively in midterm elections. Clearly, to assess these explanations or develop others, we need to face the larger problem of measurement. We need to develop measures of an expected or average vote against which to measure the short-term effects.

Votes or Seats

Part of the problem of the midterm may be an artificial one, created by the use of a misleading measure. In studying American elections, people usually look to the votes cast, or the vote margin, but the midterm results are interpreted by the seats gained or lost in the legislature. Yet the number of seats gained or lost for a party is a highly *relative* measure *depending entirely on the number of seats held before the election.* Seats are gained or lost in relation to the number of seats held before. It follows that the more seats held by one of the two American parties before the election, the larger the loss will appear after the election, even if nothing else happens or is changed at all. An identical electorate could vote in a presidential year and off year. There could be the same vote margin in the same districts in two off-year elections. But if the seats held before the election were different, the loss or gain recorded would be different as well. This effect, it is important to note, has nothing to do with the change or surge and decline of electorates. It is not a swing of the pendulum or automatic adjustment in electoral behavior, but a swing or adjustment created by the measure itself. The measure dictates this relative and compensatory effect.

The problem is compounded by focusing attention only at the midterm election and not at both presidential and midterm years. As a matter of historical fact, in the nearly 100-year period from 1880 through 1978, the president's party has lost seats in every midterm election but one (1934), and the newly elected president's party has gained seats in every presidential-year election but four. The midterm loss of seats is only one-half of the curiosity that needs to be explained.

Table 7-4   Seats, Votes, and the Normal Vote in House Elections

Year	Party of President[1]	Seats Held (Democratic)	Seats Gained or Lost (President's Party)[2]		Democratic Vote	
			Presidential Year	Off Year	% Two-Party Vote	Deviation from Normal Vote[3]
1948	Democratic	263	+75		53.2	0.8 R
1950		234		−29	50.0	4.0 R
1952	Republican	211	+22		49.9	4.1 R
1954		232		−18	52.5	1.5 R
1956	Republican	233	− 3		51.0	3.0 R
1958		284		−47	56.0	2.0 D
1960	Democratic	263	−21		54.8	0.8 D
1962		258		− 5	52.5	1.5 R
1964	Democratic	295	+37		57.3	3.3 D
1966		247		−48	51.3	2.7 R
1968	Republican	243	+ 5		50.9	3.1 R
1970		254		−12	54.4	0.4 D
1972	Republican	239	+12		52.7	1.3 R
1974		291		−48	58.5	4.5 D
1976	Democratic	292	+ 1		56.9	2.9 D
1978		276		−16	54.4	0.4 D
1980	Republican	243	+33		51.4	2.6 R
(1948-1978)	mean = 257 seats				mean = 53.5%	
	s. = 24				s. = 2.3	

[1] In presidential-year elections, the "president's party" is the party of the winning presidential candidate.

[2] Republican gains or losses are based on the number of Republican seats reported in Appendix Table A-2 on p. 144.

[3] Based on the normal vote calculated to be 54 percent Democratic. For an alternative measure, see footnote 15. R and D indicate the party favored by the deviation.

SOURCE: Democratic seats held are taken from Bureau of the Census, *Statistical Abstract of the United States* (Washington, D.C.: U.S. Government Printing Office, 1979), p. 507. The nationwide House vote is supplied by Clerk of the House of Representatives, *Statistics of the Presidential and Congressional Election*, biennial reports, 1948-1978.

The differences between the various measures used in interpreting election results are sharply outlined in Table 7-4. The table lists the seats held, the seats gained or lost, and the nationwide percentage of the

Democratic vote cast for House candidates. The table also lists the deviation from the normal vote, taken as 54 percent Democratic for the years under examination. Behind the dramatic reversals in seats gained and lost, one finds a very stable vote. There is a mean of 53.5, close to the normal vote baseline, and an extremely small standard deviation of 2.3 percentage points. The actual vote in most elections remains close to the normal vote: that is, *it is close to the vote we would expect if there were no nationwide short-term effects favoring either party in the elections,* effects such as presidential popularity or economic dissatisfactions.[15]

Table 7-4 can help us interpret the results of individual elections, compare elections to each other, and identify the deviant cases. The 1970 results, measured by seats lost, were interpreted by some as "better than average" for a midterm election while 1978 was called "about average." By the normal vote analysis, however, the results for the two elections are the same. The years 1950 and 1952 show the strongest pro-Republican voting, and 1964 (the Johnson presidential election landslide) and 1974 (the post-Watergate election) the strongest pro-Democratic voting. Other years show few short-term effects favoring either party.

One final point implicit in the table is elaborated more fully in Table 7-5. While the actual vote is close to the normal vote in both presidential-year and off-year elections, the short-term effects that do exist are different. *They help the president's party in the presidential year and hurt the party in the off year.* In the presidential-election years, seven of the eight cases (all but 1948) show deviations in favor of the president's party. In the off years, six of eight cases (all but 1954 and

Table 7-5 Deviations from the Normal Vote in Presidential-Year and Off-Year Elections, 1948-1978

	Elections	
	Presidential Year	*Off Year*
Mean Deviation from Normal Vote[1]	2.4	2.1
Mean Net Deviation from Normal Vote (for or against President's Party)[2]	+2.2	−1.7

[1] Ignoring the signs; i.e., whether the deviation is in a pro-Democratic or pro-Republican direction in Table 7-2.

[2] Taking the difference between the total deviation in favor of the president's party and the total deviation against the president's party, and then taking the average for the eight off-year and presidential-year elections.

1978) show deviations opposing the president's party. On the average, for the elections from 1948 through 1978, the president's party gains two percentage points in the vote in short-term effects from the presidential-election year and loses two percentage points in the off year.

Looking at votes rather than seats is useful in several respects. It provides a measure for short-term effects; it shows that these effects occur in both presidential and off years; and it leads to sharply different interpretations for some elections. Why, then, are votes not used in interpreting midterm results? One reason is that House elections are held at the district—not the national—level; hence, a national House vote can itself be seen as an artificial measure. But if the interpretations made are *also* national—concerning what the voters "said" or the election "meant" for the president and party in the White House—then an equivalent national measure seems the correct one, whether one totals the number of seats won or lost or the percentage of votes cast. Of course, if one's concern is interpreting district-level results, then one still needs votes, and some calculation of the expected vote, at the district level.

A more serious objection to the measure is raised by the difficulty of calculation. Seats are easily counted on election night, ready for instant analysis and the next day's news. Votes, by contrast, require totalling the results from 435 districts. But if the two measures give very different results, and one can be seriously questioned, then such calculation may be necessary.

An Alternative Measure of Seats

Alternatively, if one still prefers to use seats as a measure, one can easily calculate the average number of seats held for a party for any given time period and see if the seats won in an election are above or below average. For example, from 1948 to 1978 the Democratic party held a mean number of House seats of 257 with a standard deviation of 24. From 1960 to 1978, the Democrats held a mean of 266 seats with a standard deviation of 20. From these results, one can then calculate whether any particular election result was above or below average and which results were exceptional in being more than one standard deviation from the mean: for example, more than 281 Democratic seats or less than 233 from 1948 through 1978. The standard deviation, in fact, can provide even more information of interest. Since it supplies a measure of the variation around the mean, it tells us the number of seats, in any one time period, that might be expected to change from one party to the other. A standard deviation of 24 indicates that typically 24 seats might change parties. A change from a standard deviation of 24 to 20 suggests an increased resistance to change—in other words, the increased safeness of House seats discussed at length in Chapter 3.

Table 7-6   Seats Won or Lost by the President's Party Compared to the Average Number of Seats Held*, 1948-1980

Year	Democratic Seats	President's Party	Seats Held by President's Party Compared to Average Number (mean=257 Democratic seats)
Off-Year Elections			
1950	234	Democratic	Less
1954	232	Republican	More
1958	284	Republican	Less
1962	258	Democratic	More
1966	247	Democratic	Less
1970	254	Republican	More
1974	291	Republican	Less
1978	276	Democratic	More
Presidential-Year Elections			
1948	263	Democratic	More
1952	211	Republican	More
1956	233	Republican	More
1960	263	Democratic	More
1964	295	Democratic	More
1968	243	Republican	More
1972	239	Republican	More
1976	292	Democratic	More
(1980)	(243)	(Republican)	(More)

*In presidential-year elections, the "president's party" is the party of the winning presidential candidate. The 1980 results, reported in parentheses, can be compared against the past 30 years when the mean was 257 and the standard deviation 24.

SOURCE: Calculated by the author. Democratic seats held are taken from Bureau of the Census, *Statistical Abstract of the United States* (Washington, D.C.: U.S. Government Printing Office, 1979), p. 507. See Appendix Table A-2 on page 144 for the number of Republican seats in Congress since 1948.

Use of this alternative measure from Table 7-4 gives the results as summarized in Table 7-6. Of the eight midterm elections from 1950 to 1978, four show the president's party winning less than the average number of Democratic seats (257) and four show the president's party winning more than the average. Of the nine presidential-election years, all show the victorious presidential candidate's party winning more than the average. In effect, the measure indicates that the midterm election results are only one part, and perhaps the less interesting part, of the variation in House seats from one election to another.

This measure has the disadvantage of being derived from the very seats we are attempting to interpret and yet the advantage of being easy to calculate. The results from any one election can thus be immediately compared against the past typical pattern. In 1980, for example, the Democrats lost 33 House seats, a fact interpreted by many to mean that the House, along with the Senate and White House, had undergone a dramatic change. Table 7-4, however, places 1980 House results squarely within the average range. In line with the past eight presidential-election years, the party of the winning presidential candidate—the Republican party—won more than the average number of House seats. Also in line with the past, the Democrats would hold 243 seats, close to the average figure of 257 and identical to the seats held after the Republican presidential victory in 1968. When the 97th Congress convened, the House had the same number of Democrats as the House which debated the president's conduct of the Vietnam war, and almost the same number (239) as the House which initiated impeachment proceedings in early 1974.

Both measures—the national vote and the average seats held—point to a stability in House voting little affected by presidential or other national trends. The seats gained in one year are lost in another. Looking only at the gains or losses obscures the overall effect. Moreover, it is a small number of seats that shifts between the parties. Three-fourths of the 193 Democratic seats held in 1972 and not subsequently redistricted stayed Democratic throughout the decade and remained in Democratic hands after 1980. Of the 52 seats lost, 5 were lost in 1974, 10 in 1975 or 1976, 15 in 1978, and 22 in 1980.[16] Of all 361 House seats not redistricted after 1972, *only 19—or 5 percent—changed party more than once throughout the decade* (from the 1972 through the 1980 election). These seats changed party once and then changed back again across the four elections. No districts changed party three or four times. Overall, the rate of party change across the decade for the 361 unredistricted seats is as follows:

> 67 percent did not change parties;
> 27 percent changed parties once;
> 5 percent changed parties twice;
> 0 percent changed more than twice.

From the Republican landslide presidential elections in 1972 through Watergate to the Reagan sweep in 1980, a large majority of House seats stayed with the same party.

This stability accords with the results of the preceding chapters. Both party voting and incumbency, within the context of voters' low information about congressional candidates, insulate the House from short-term national trends. Of course, there are occasions when short-term effects can add as much as four percentage points nationwide for one party's House candidates—for example, the presidential-year election of 1964 or the midterm election of 1974. The measures, therefore, can also clarify when such occasions do and do not occur.

ANOTHER LOOK AT THE MIDTERM ELECTION

This analysis suggests two points of importance. First, most congressional elections hold close to a normal vote—or the vote expected if there were no nationwide short-term effects at all. The dramatic reversals in seats won and lost disappear when we look at the voting results. Overall, the president's party gains about two percentage points of the vote in the presidential year and loses the same in the off year. The dramatic shifts also disappear when we look at the average number of seats held for a party over time and the very small standard deviation. This relatively small effect is found in the survey results as well, where presidential evaluations and party ties, compared to other influences, rank low in importance. In short, when we expand our perspective to both presidential years and off years and look beyond the relative measure of seats gained or lost, much of the mystery of the midterm election disappears.

Second, we do find some positive effects for the president's party in the presidential-election year and some negative effects in the off year. Both the coattail and negative voting arguments appear to have identified one-half of a larger pattern of House voting and missed the other half. This pattern suggests some slight short-term influences in congressional elections connected to the president or the party in the White House. How they are connected, however, in the perception of the voters is still not clear from the survey results.

The more interesting mystery concerns why even these small effects are present and how perceptions of the president or president's party become translated by the individual citizen into a congressional vote. Neither coattail nor negative voting arguments offer satisfactory explanations. We appear to be dealing with three cognitive components—a perception of events (concerning the president, the administration, the economy, etc.); a short-term perception of party; and a connection between that party perception and the party of the congressional candidate:

| Perception of Events | ➡ | Perception of Party | ➡ | Perception of Congressional Candidates |

The links between these perceptions, however, are not clear. Short-term party perceptions may be highly influenced by presidential perceptions, but, as we saw earlier, party cues do not appear to help identify the issue stands of congressional candidates. People could not say they liked or disliked House challengers for reasons involving their party ties, judging by the very small number of responses given to the open-ended questions. The first step in the cognitive linkage, the one between president and party, is easier to make than the second.

We also do not know whether these cognitive connections, whatever they may be, are made by all voters or only some specific portion. Perhaps some kinds of voters more than others use presidential and short-term party perceptions, depending on partisanship, general levels of information and interest, or relative information about presidential and congressional affairs. More work is needed, too, on the differences, if any, between presidential-year and off-year voters. Panel surveys have been conducted that ask the same citizens over a number of years about their voting behavior. We should therefore be able to trace changes in perceptions and turnout across a sequence of presidential and off-year elections. Future surveys might ask people directly about the role and relevance of the president in congressional elections. Further analysis of past surveys is also indicated. It is ironic that the one election (1974) where negative presidential voting might best be identified was the one election where a survey concentrated on Senate questions. Nevertheless, open-ended questions in 1974 for Senate races and in other years for House races should yield more information.

SUMMARY

If elections are indeed "meaningful democratic acts,"[17] then we need to know what they mean and be able to interpret them when they occur. The midterm election puzzle thus becomes a useful illustration for this final empirical chapter. To interpret these elections, we can draw on the material and perspective of the preceding chapters. We can measure short-term forces and recognize the importance of other congressional effects.

Analysis leads beyond the surface of the wide swings in seats gained and lost to the essential stability of the House vote. Most elections—presidential-year and off-year—hold close to a normal vote—what would be expected if there were no nationwide short-term forces operating in the election. Some deviations occur benefiting the president's party in the presidential year and hurting it in the off-year, but these are small at all times and, in some elections, nonexistent. The results from surveys support the aggregate results. When voters' partisanship is fully controlled for, much of the effect of presidential approval or disapproval disappears. Studies of defections from party lines need to watch for the hidden incumbency effects. Evaluations of the congressional candidates—in terms of their personal qualities, experience, and leadership as well as their issue positions—appear more important than presidential evaluations.

The preoccupation with presidential elections has extended even to the midterm election. Assuming no information about congressional candidates on the part of the voters, writers have turned to the presidency to understand the House results. But once congressional factors are measured and introduced into the analysis, the importance of the presidential influence is greatly reduced.

Nevertheless, some systematic, although small, effects of presidential party voting in both the presidential-year and off-year elections can be discerned. Some voters appear to be using either presidential or presidential-party cues in making a congressional voting decision. But we do not know who these voters are or how they can be distinguished from other voters, how this information is translated and applied, or how much of it is caused by shifts in turnout between the two kinds of elections. At the end of this final empirical chapter, several unanswered questions remain.

NOTES

1. See V. O. Key, Jr., *Parties, Politics and Pressure Groups*, 5th ed. (New York: Thomas Y. Crowell & Co., 1964); Angus Campbell, "Voters and Elections: Past and Present," *Journal of Politics* (November 1964): 745-757, and Campbell "Surge and Decline: A Study of Electoral Change," *Public Opinion Quarterly* (Fall 1960): 397-418; and Milton Cummings, Jr., *Congressmen and the Electorate* (New York: Free Press, 1966).
2. Campbell, "Surge and Decline."
3. See Herbert Kritzer and Robert Eubank, "Presidential Coattails Revisited: Partisanship and Incumbency Effects," *American Journal of Political Science* (August 1979): 615-626; George Edwards, "The Impact of Presidential Coattails on Outcomes of Congressional Elections," *American Politics Quarterly* (January 1979): 94-108. Note, however, that coattails may be hidden and not obvious from the presidential election results. See Gary Jacobson, "Presidential Coattails in 1972," *Public Opinion Quarterly* (Summer 1976): 194-200; and Stan Kaplowitz, "Using Aggregate Voting Data to Measure Presidential Coattail Effects," *Public Opinion Quarterly* (Fall 1971): 415-419.
4. Robert Arseneau and Raymond Wolfinger, "Voting Behavior in Congressional Elections" (Paper presented at the annual meeting of the American Political Science Association, New Orleans, Louisiana, September 4-8, 1973).
5. Samuel Kernell, "Presidential Popularity and Negative Voting: An Alternative Explanation of the Midterm Congressional Decline of the President's Party," *American Political Science Review* (March 1977): 62.
6. Edward Tufte, "Determinants of the Outcomes of Midterm Congressional Elections," *American Political Science Review* (September 1975): 812-826.

7. See, for example, Francisco Arcelus and Allen Meltzer, "The Effect of Aggregate Economic Variables on Congressional Elections," *American Political Science Review* (December 1975): 1232-1239; Gerald Kramer, "Short Run Fluctuations in U.S. Voting Behavior, 1896-1964," *American Political Science Review* (March 1971): 131-143; Susan Lepper, "Voting Behavior and Aggregate Policy Targets," *Public Choice* (Summer 1974): 67-82; and Richard Li, "Public Policy and Short-Term Fluctuations in U.S. Voting Behavior," *Political Methodology* (Winter 1976): 49-70.

8. John Mueller, "Presidential Popularity from Truman to Johnson," *American Political Science Review* (March 1970): 18-24.

9. Donald Kinder and D. Roderick Kiewiet, "Economic Discontent and Political Behavior: The Role of Personal Grievances and Collective Economic Judgments in Congressional Voting," *American Journal of Political Science* (August 1979): 495-527.

10. Morris Fiorina, "Economic Retrospective Voting in American National Elections," *American Journal of Political Science* (May 1978): 426-433. See also James Kuklinski and Darrell West, "Economic Expectations and Mass Voting in United States House and Senate Elections," *American Political Science Review* (June 1981). Kuklinski and West find some slight relationship for Senate voting, but none for House voting.

11. James Piereson, "Presidential Popularity and Midterm Voting at Different Electoral Levels," *American Journal of Political Science* (November 1975): 688, 689.

12. See Albert Cover's analysis of incumbency and party defections discussed in Chapter 4 of this volume.

13. Lyn Ragsdale, "The Fiction of Congressional Elections as Presidential Events," *American Politics Quarterly* (October 1980):375-398.

14. The results are based on an ordinary least squares regression against the vote. The relative strength of the variables as predictors of the vote is seen by the standardized regression coefficients. The candidate evaluation questions were asked only for the House in 1978 and the Senate in 1974.

15. Another analysis shows similar results to those reported in Tables 7-4 and 7-5. See Warren Miller et al., *American National Election Studies Data Sourcebook, 1952-1978* (Cambridge: Harvard University Press, 1980), p. 379. The authors calculate a normal, or expected, vote for each election. The figures range from 52.7 to 58.5 for 1956-1978. Most of the years show results quite close to those of Table 7-4. The overall results are similar to those in Table 7-5, showing an average deviation for presidential years of 2.85 percentage points and for off years of 3.40. The deviations in the presidential years favor the president's party and in the off years the opposing party.

16. For the 1972-1978 results, see *America Votes 13*, ed. Richard M. Scammon and Alice V. McGillivray (Washington, D.C.: Congressional Quarterly, 1979). For 1980 results, see *Congressional Quarterly Weekly Report*, November 8, 1980. Note that even the redistricted seats do not show much partisan change. The two states completely redistricted after 1972 were California and Texas. Texas had 20 Democrats in the delegation in 1972 before redistricting and 19 Democrats after the 1980 election; California had 23 Democrats before and 22 Democrats after.

17. See the remark by Gerald Pomper and discussion in Chapter 6.

8

Congressional Elections and Future Research

In studying congressional elections, we go beyond the spotlight of the presidential contest to an arena that receives much less research attention. The results of these elections shape the laws and major policies of the nation and pose implications for the American democracy beyond who wins and who loses in House and Senate races. This study, then, seeks to bring together and extend the initial work on the subject.

Models of voting behavior, drawn from presidential elections, assume (1) information about both major candidates in the competition, and (2) that the uninterested citizen does not vote. In voting beyond the presidential level, both assumptions can be questioned. On the first Tuesday after the first Monday in November, in even-numbered years, American citizens elect their major governing representatives. They elect presidents and representatives and state judges and coroners. According to the democratic ideal, citizens will weigh information about the candidates in making a voting decision. The winners are "the people's choice" and thus are legitimized in the work they do and the decisions they make. Nevertheless, the presidential contest, which alone has been the subject of serious study, may be almost alone in meeting these democratic expectations. The prime-time televised debate between two presidential candidates is the extreme exception in American politics, and so those who would understand these politics must broaden their focus of attention.

In contrast to previous models, this study assumes that elections may include some portion of citizens uninterested in the office they are voting for and without information on at least one of the major party candidates in the race. Voting is only one of many selections people are called upon to make. In making these selections, people can apply general rules or specific information, and they must calculate the costs of applying one kind of decision rule as opposed to the other. So, in any election contest, some voters will follow the competitive model and weigh specific information about both candidates, but we cannot assume that all voters will do this or that we know what proportion will. Therefore, to explain elections and to compare elections across time and across offices, we should look at the amount and kind of information available. When and under what conditions does information get across to voters? What proportion of voters recognizes one, none, or both candidates in a race? What kind of general-choice decisions can substitute for more specific information? This view of elections emphasizes information—not competition. Information is critical in determining when and under what conditions the competitive ideal can be realized.

V. O. Key has observed that:

> Voters are not fools. . . . The electorate behaves about as rationally and responsibly as we should expect, given the clarity of the alternatives presented to it and the character of the information available to it.[1]

The first four words are widely quoted, but the second half of the observation, rarely included in the quotation, may be equally important. The information available to the voters will affect the kind of choices they can make.

INFORMATION AND CONGRESSIONAL VOTING

In congressional races, information varies with the office contested and the kind of candidate. Senate candidates are visible enough for their names to be recognized and to be cited for their contact with voters. People have had "some contact with" or "learned something about" the two competing candidates. In many House races, in contrast, voters know one but not the other of the competitors: the incumbents are known and the challengers are not. In these races, less than half of the voters recognized the challenger's name when it was supplied to them. Far fewer could give reasons for liking or disliking these candidates. So, in House races, less than half of the voters could claim to know something about both candidates. Models based on a weighing of preference between two candidates cannot explain these voters' decisions.

Candidate visibility varies, and visibility affects the vote. We thus need to inquire about conditions in the political environment affecting the amount of information about the candidates. Campaign spending and media coverage can be shown to help the challenger—not the incumbent. These effects appear to increase the recognition of the candidates disadvantaged in visibility at the start. Once their disadvantage is removed, the candidates can campaign more equally in making their qualifications known. Nevertheless, the relationship between spending or media coverage and electoral success is by no means a simple one. Success draws money, and money helps success. A race perceived to be safe, in either the Senate or House, will attract little money or media attention, and these effects reinforce the original safeness. Whereas most House challengers spend less than their incumbent-opponents—and receive less from campaign contributions—challengers running against the most vulnerable incumbents will frequently spend more. The vulnerability or the safeness is thus part cause and part effect. Given this reinforcing circle, members of Congress may need to do more than win re-election: they may need to win it so substantially in any one year that they discourage opposition the next time around.

The importance and the variability of information can help explain key influences on congressional voting. Comparing the different effects of incumbency in the Senate and House, we find two factors at work simultaneously. House incumbents succeed in communicating a positive impression—as competent, trusted, and concerned about the district—while their opponents succeed in communicating little information of any kind. Senate incumbents also communicate a positive impression. Indeed, few congressional candidates are perceived negatively. Senators, however, must compete with their opponents' communication: the information about challengers is sufficient to provide alternatives for the voters' decisions. Party labels, like a candidate's incumbency, provide low-cost information to voters. A vote in accord with one's party affiliation, like a vote for a candidate in office, is a way of making a choice with very little information. In 1978 contests between incumbents and challengers—and these were the large majority of all contests—only 15 percent of Senate voters and only 13 percent of House voters cast votes not in accord with party or incumbency cues.

More specific information, of course, does get across to voters. Both the qualifications of candidates and their issue positions can affect the vote beyond the effects of party and incumbency. Congressional candidate preferences are found to be considerably more important than presidential preferences in Senate and House contests. And in the House, although not in the Senate, candidate preferences are more important than party identification. Senators are liked and disliked for a variety of reasons resembling those cited for governors and presidents, while representatives are mainly referred to in terms of generally favorable personal characteristics. Nevertheless, simply knowing the party of the incumbent is as good a predictor of the vote in House races as knowing which candidate is preferred. Similarly, issues can be shown to exert an independent influence on the vote. Both aggregate and survey studies can demonstrate this effect. At the same time, it is important to remember the proportion of voters involved. Less than one-third of the people who themselves have positions on issues can place the congressional candidates on the issues. Fewer still report preferring one candidate more than another because of a campaign issue or an issue of importance to them, and most of those who do, prefer the incumbent. Indeed, incumbents are preferred and voted for by these "issue voters" in about the same proportion as the electorate as a whole.

These results have implications for representation in Congress and for the future of electoral competition. Until recently, research attention has focused on incumbents in the House and on what they must be doing right to be so solidly re-elected. Constituency service, district visits, bureaucratic errand running, office support—all were cited to explain the incumbents' electoral success. Re-election became *de facto* the sign of successful representation. Broadening attention to the challengers and the Senate comparative results leads to somewhat less sanguine conclusions. In Senate races, voters choose between two candidates they recognize and have had some contact with. The minimum conditions for competition between candidates are present. In House races, however, these necessary conditions are not present. Indeed, it is difficult to avoid the conclusion that many House incumbents win by default.

One can see in the Senate pattern the possible future of House races. Incumbents, perceived to be safe, discourage strong opposition, contributions for the challenger, and media attention. However, this reinforcing circle of safeness, cut for the Senate, can be cut for the House, with increased interest group support and spending for the challenger's campaign. There are already indications that such a trend is under way. Nationally organized groups have funded strong opposition for previously safe liberal House Democrats. House leaders in 1980, again predominantly liberal Democrats, faced strong and very well-funded opposition. While there have been fewer attempts by liberal groups to unseat safe conservative representatives, such counterorganization would seem a logical and necessary response. Yet these effects, too, raise many potential problems. They might tie representatives too closely to interest group or ideological politics and thus create a new kind of political debate. If the strongest liberals are opposed by the strongest conservatives, with both groups supported by their respective political action committees, then one would have "competition," but it would be of a kind much more extreme and ideological than in the past. The impact of any such changes—for the House and for popular representation—will deserve some careful attention.

The results also raise questions about the centrality of voters to the election results. Voters can use specific information, but other points in the political context determine when such information will be available and what qualifications and issues are raised. Other points determine who gets the choice for the open-seat race, whether two candidates or one is recognized, and how strong the competition will be.

These findings are internally consistent, viewed from the standpoint of how people make selections, and they suggest a range of electoral behavior beyond the presidential contest that is important to recognize. The American voter is not adequately described as a presidential voter, nor are the communications to this voter—from the candidates, the campaign, the incumbent's activity, or the news media—the same for congressional as for presidential contests.

The findings can also begin to correct the considerable misinformation on the subject found in popular commentary and often shared by the candidates themselves. People cite House incumbents' institutional support to explain their success at the polls. Office salaries, visits home, and other benefits are extensively catalogued. Yet Senate incumbents enjoy the same institutional support without the same electoral success. The personal contact between representative and voters is also cited as a reason for success, but personal contact, we find, makes no difference to the vote. While very high proportions of voters having personal contact with the incumbent do, in fact, vote for the incumbent, equally high proportions of voters not having this contact also vote for the incumbent.

Writers refer to "split-ticket voting" and the increase in party defections to suggest that congressional voters are becoming more informed about candidates or concerned about the issues. However, there is no evidence to suggest a change in House voters' information over the 30 years of survey studies, and the "new breed" of Independent voters are as likely to support House incumbents as the party identifiers are. In addition, the increased party defection can be traced to the effects of incumbency. No increase in defections is found for voters in open-seat contests. A candidate's age or sex is frequently cited as an electorally relevant characteristic, posing an advantage or disadvantage in the campaign, but overall the age or sex of the candidate makes no difference to the vote.

Every off-year election brings a storm of commentary about the past two years of the presidential administration and about what the House voters have "said" about the president. But none of the commentaries compares the results against a normal vote or sees them as part of a larger oscillation involving presidential-year elections. We find, in fact, that most House elections hold close to a stable vote, with about two percentage points in vote margin on the average gained for the president's party in the presidential-election year and two percentage points lost in the off-year.

THE FUTURE OF CONGRESSIONAL ELECTION RESEARCH

Nevertheless, the studies presently available represent a very early stage in political science research. For each question considered, a number of other questions are raised. Whole topic areas remain virtually unexamined: for example, the processes of recruitment, or the variation and impact of campaigns. Even the present findings are tentative and require further study. Consequently, at this point it should be useful to review some of the major questions remaining unanswered and the kind of work that needs to be done.

A first attempt was made to examine how voters' information varies by type of race and type of candidate and how it is affected by other influences in the political environment. The preliminary results for the Senate and House need extending and comparison with other offices. At this point, we do not know whether information should be seen as essentially dichotomous or continuous—that is, whether there is "sufficient" information (as in presidential and some Senate contests) for voters to compare two competing candidates as opposed to insufficient information; or whether there are degrees of information that need to be distinguished. Are House races, for example, like the races for state judgeships and unlike the presidential contest, or are there further degrees of information that should be identified? Surveys have only begun to use the name recognition question that supplies people with the candidate's name as in the voting booth. These questions need repeating in future surveys and further analysis. The beginning studies of spending need to be extended and the very first studies of media impact need much more attention. These are topics of constant speculation, but the words spent on them are far in excess of the facts known. More fundamentally, we do know how citizens themselves see the information needed and used for a voting decision; how people get and use political information; when and under what conditions a search for further information is undertaken. We do not know how or to what extent communication from the campaign is received by voters. Research designs have not yet linked the campaign stimulus with the voter response.

We have begun to compile basic data about attitudes toward incumbents, but the findings remain tentative until we extend the Senate-House comparisons. At minimum, it will be necessary to ask open-ended questions about likes and dislikes for both Senate and House incumbents in the same election year and among the same sample of citizens. Speculations about why House incumbents are so strongly supported must remain speculations until tested against the Senate comparative results. What we now know about incumbents is drawn heavily from one 1978 survey study. These results require repetition and corroboration for other election years, and they require comparison between presidential-year and off-year elections.

Beyond these obvious needs, it might be helpful to distinguish between serious and token races by challengers and to study the preliminary processes determining which shall occur. A sizable portion of challengers opposing safe incumbents spend virtually no money on the campaign, in the process amassing less than 20 percent of the vote. Distinguishing such token challengers from others might be a useful first step toward a taxonomy of House races.

Additional effort is needed in working with aggregate data to develop ways of measuring short-term effects. Hypotheses about candidate qualifications, presidential coattails, interest group support, and issues or campaign strategy require some measure of impact beyond partisanship and incumbency. Currently, these remain untested and in the realm of journalistic speculation, but we know little about congressional elections until we can measure such effects. Both aggregate and contextual data will need more systematic analysis to incorporate that information with the developing knowledge from survey results.

Even the studies already conducted need to be extended. It will be important to see the variation across election years, depending on issues and events and the presence or absence of a presidential campaign. All of the findings merit further testing across time and should become richer and clearer by such longitudinal analysis. They also require more explicit comparisons between the Senate and House and between congressional races and other contests. The American voter selects state and local officials as well as candidates for the presidency and Congress. Hence any propositions about the effects of information or the frequency of competition will need to be extended to these races.

We like to think "the people choose" and that when they speak we know what they are saying. The importance of elections rests on these two minimum assumptions. But considerable work remains before we understand the parameters of their choice, what is being said, and when—and why—there is silence.

NOTE

1. V. O. Key, Jr., *The Responsible Electorate* (Cambridge: Harvard University Press, 1966), p. 7.

Appendix

Table A-1   Turnout for Presidential and House Elections, 1932-1980

Year	Estimated Population of Voting Age	Vote Cast for Presidential Electors		Vote Cast for U.S. Representatives	
		Number	Percent	Number	Percent
1932	75,768,000	39,732,000	52.4	37,657,000	49.7
1934	77,997,000	—	—	32,256,000	41.4
1936	80,174,000	45,643,000	56.9	42,886,000	53.5
1938	82,354,000	—	—	36,236,000	44.0
1940	84,728,000	49,900,000	58.9	46,951,000	55.4
1942	86,465,000	—	—	28,074,000	32.5
1944	85,654,000	47,977,000	56.0	45,103,000	52.7
1946	92,659,000	—	—	34,398,000	37.1
1948	95,573,000	48,794,000	51.1	45,933,000	48.1
1950	98,134,000	—	—	40,342,000	41.1
1952	99,929,000	61,551,000	61.6	57,571,000	57.6
1954	102,075,000	—	—	42,580,000	41.7
1956	104,515,000	62,027,000	59.3	58,426,000	55.9
1958	106,447,000	—	—	45,818,000	43.0
1960	109,672,000	68,838,000	62.8	64,133,000	58.5
1962	112,952,000	—	—	51,267,000	45.4
1964	114,090,000	70,645,000	61.9	65,895,000	57.8
1966	116,638,000	—	—	52,908,000	45.4
1968	120,285,000	73,212,000	60.9	66,288,000	55.1
1970	124,498,000	—	—	54,173,000	43.5
1972	140,068,000	77,719,000	55.5	71,430,000	51.0
1974	145,035,000	—	—	52,495,000	36.2
1976	150,127,000	81,556,000	54.3	74,422,000	49.6
1978	155,492,000	—	—	54,693,000	35.2
1980	160,491,000	84,263,000	52.5	72,796,000	45.4

SOURCE: Bureau of the Census, *Statistical Abstract of the United States* (Washington, D.C.: U.S. Government Printing Office, 1979), p. 513. The 1980 estimated population of voting age was calculated by the Population Division, Bureau of the Census, and does not reflect 1980 Census figures. The 1980 vote totals were also compiled by the Census Bureau, which used the unofficial returns in *Congressional Quarterly Weekly Report,* November 8, 1980, pp. 3299, 3338-3345. These figures do not reflect votes cast for all of the minor parties, and votes for unopposed candidates were not included.

Table A-2 Party Control of the Presidency, Senate, House, 1901-1982

Congress	Years	President	Senate D	R	Other*	House D	R	Other*
57th	1901-1902	McKinley T. Roosevelt	31	55	4	151	197	9
58th	1903-1904	T. Roosevelt	33	57	—	178	208	—
59th	1905-1906	T. Roosevelt	33	57	—	136	250	—
60th	1907-1908	T. Roosevelt	31	61	—	164	222	—
61st	1909-1910	Taft	32	61	—	172	219	—
62nd	1911-1912	Taft	41	51	—	228	161	1
63rd	1913-1914	Wilson	51	44	1	291	127	17
64th	1915-1916	Wilson	56	40	—	230	196	9
65th	1917-1918	Wilson	53	42	—	216	210	6
66th	1919-1920	Wilson	47	49	—	190	240	3
67th	1921-1922	Harding	37	59	—	131	301	1
68th	1923-1924	Coolidge	43	51	2	205	225	5
69th	1925-1926	Coolidge	39	56	1	183	247	4
70th	1927-1928	Coolidge	46	49	1	195	237	3
71st	1929-1930	Hoover	39	56	1	167	267	1
72nd	1931-1932	Hoover	47	48	1	220	214	1
73rd	1933-1934	F. Roosevelt	60	35	1	310	117	5
74th	1935-1936	F. Roosevelt	69	25	2	319	103	10
75th	1937-1938	F. Roosevelt	76	16	4	331	89	13
76th	1939-1940	F. Roosevelt	69	23	4	261	164	4
77th	1941-1942	F. Roosevelt	66	28	2	268	162	5

*Excludes vacancies at beginning of each session.

**The 437 members of the House in the 86th and 87th Congresses is attributable to the at-large representative given to both Alaska (January 3, 1959) and Hawaii (August 21, 1959) prior to redistricting in 1962.

Congress	Years	President	Senate D	Senate R	Senate Other*	House D	House R	House Other*
78th	1943-1944	F. Roosevelt	58	37	1	218	208	4
79th	1945-1946	Truman	56	38	1	242	190	2
80th	1947-1948	Truman	45	51	—	188	245	1
81st	1949-1950	Truman	54	42	—	263	171	1
82nd	1951-1952	Truman	49	47	—	234	199	1
83rd	1953-1954	Eisenhower	47	48	1	211	221	1
84th	1955-1956	Eisenhower	48	47	1	232	203	—
85th	1957-1958	Eisenhower	49	47	—	233	200	—
86th**	1959-1960	Eisenhower	65	35	—	284	153	—
87th**	1961-1962	Kennedy	65	35	—	263	174	—
88th	1963-1964	Kennedy Johnson	67	33	—	258	177	—
89th	1965-1966	Johnson	68	32	—	295	140	—
90th	1967-1968	Johnson	64	36	—	247	187	—
91st	1969-1970	Nixon	57	43	—	243	192	—
92nd	1971-1972	Nixon	54	44	2	254	180	—
93rd	1973-1974	Nixon Ford	56	42	2	239	192	1
94th	1975-1976	Ford	60	37	2	291	144	—
95th	1977-1978	Carter	61	38	1	292	143	—
96th	1979-1980	Carter	58	41	1	276	157	—
97th	1981-1982	Reagan	46	53	1	243	192	—

☐ Republican Control   ☐ Democratic Control

SOURCE: Bureau of the Census, *Statistical Abstract of the United States* (Washington, D.C.: U.S. Government Printing Office, 1979), p. 507 and *Members of Congress Since 1789*, 2nd ed. (Washington, D.C.: Congressional Quarterly, 1981), pp. 176-177.

Table A-3   Seats that Changed Party in the House and Senate, 1954-1980

Year	Total Changes*	Incumbent Defeated D to R	Incumbent Defeated D to R	Open Seat D to R	Open Seat D to R
House Seats					
1954	26	3	18	2	3
1956	20	7	7	2	4
1958	50	1	35	0	14
1960	37	23	2	6	6
1962	19	9	5	2	3
1964	57	5	39	5	8
1966	47	39	1	4	3
1968	11	5	0	2	4
1970	25	2	9	6	8
1972	23	6	3	9	5
1974	55	4	36	2	13
1976	22	7	5	3	7
1978	33	14	5	8	6
1980	39	27	3	8	1
Senate Seats					
1954	8	2	4	1	1
1956	8	1	3	3	1
1958	13	0	11	0	2
1960	2	1	0	1	0
1962	8	2	3	0	3
1964	4	1	3	0	0
1966	3	1	0	2	0
1968	9	4	0	3	2
1970	6	3	2	1	0
1972	10	1	4	3	2
1974	6	0	2	1	3
1976	14	5	4	2	3
1978	13	5	2	3	3
1980	12	9	0	3	0

*The total number of switched seats out of 435 seats in the House and 33 or 34 seats in the Senate.

SOURCE: John Bibby et al., *Vital Statistics on Congress, 1980* (Washington, D.C.: American Enterprise Institute, 1980), pp. 9, 11. © 1980 by American Enterprise Institute. *Congressional Quarterly Weekly Report,* November 8, 1980, p. 3302 and January 3, 1981, p. 5.

NOTE: The table reports shifts in party control of seats from immediately before to immediately after the November election. It does not include party shifts as a result of redistricting.

Table A-4 Senate Incumbent Losers and Winners, 1974-1980

Incumbent	Age[1]	Years in Senate[2]	Age	Elective Office[3]	Spending[4]
			Challenger		
Losers					
1974					
Dominick (R-Colo.)	59	12	36	—	
Cook (R-Ky.)	48	6	50	Gov.	
1976					
Tunney (D-Calif.)	42	6	70	—	less
Hartke (D-Ind.)	57	18	59	—	more
Beall (R-Md.)	49	6	43	Rep.	more
Montoya (D-N.M.)	61	12	41	—	less
Buckley (C/R-N.Y.)	53	6	49	—	less
Taft (R-Ohio)	59	6	59	Sen.	less
Brock (R-Tenn.)	45	6	45	—	less
Moss (D-Utah)	65	18	42		more
McGee (D-Wyo.)	61	18	43	—	more
1978					
Haskell (D-Colo.)	62	6	41	Rep.	more
Clark (D-Iowa)	49	6	49	—	less
Hathaway (D-Maine)	54	6	38	Rep.	more
Brooke (R-Mass.)	59	12	37	Rep.	less
Griffin (R-Mich.)	55	12	44	—	less
McIntyre (D-N.H.)	63	18	37	—	more
1980					
Talmadge (D-Ga.)	67	18+	49	—	less
Church (D-Idaho)	56	18+	42	Rep.	less
Bayh (D-Ind.)	52	18	33	Rep.	less
Culver (D-Iowa)	48	6	47	Rep.	more
Durkin (D-N.H.)	44	5	49	—	less
Morgan (D-N.C.)	55	6	49	—	more
McGovern (D-S.D.)	58	18	57	Rep.	less
Magnuson (D-Wash.)	75	18+	52	—	less
Nelson (D-Wis.)	64	18	38	Rep.	less
Winners					
1974					
Allen (D-Ala.)	61	6	Unopposed		
Gravel (D-Alaska)	44	6	57	—	
Goldwater (R-Ariz.)	65	18	50	—	
Cranston (D-Calif.)	60	6	46	—	
Ribicoff (D-Conn.)	64	12	33	—	
Talmadge (D-Ga.)	61	18	35	—	

Table A-4 (Continued)

Incumbent	Age[1]	Years in Senate[2]	Challenger		
			Age	Elective Office[3]	Spending[4]
Inouye (D-Hawaii)	50	12	Unopposed		
Church (D-Idaho)	50	18	43	—	
Stevenson (D-Ill.)	43	4	52	—	
Bayh (D-Ind.)	46	12	42	—	
Dole (R-Kan.)	51	6	48	Rep.	
Long (D-La.)	51	18+	Unopposed		
Mathias (R-Md.)	52	6	38	—	
Eagleton (D-Mo.)	45	6	63	Rep.	
Javits (R-N.Y.)	70	18	46		
Young (R-N.D.)	76	18+	54	Gov.	
Bellmon (R-Okla.)	53	6	55	Rep.	
Packwood (R-Ore.)	42	6	51	—	
Schweicker (R-Pa.)	48	6	48	—	
Hollings (D-S.C.)	52	8	43	—	
McGovern (D-S.D.)	52	12	42	—	
Magnuson (D-Wash.)	69	18+	46	—	
Nelson (D-Wis.)	58	12	34	—	
1976					
Weicker (R-Conn.)	45	6	46	—	less
Roth (R-Del.)	55	6	34	—	less
Chiles (D-Fla.)	46	6	46	—	more
Muskie (D-Maine)	62	18	42	—	more
Kennedy (D-Mass.)	44	14	41	—	less
Humphrey (D-Minn.)	65	18+	54	—	less
Stennis (D-Miss.)	75	18+	Unopposed		
Cannon (D-Nev.)	64	18	39	Rep.	less
Harrison (D-N.J.)	56	18+	39	—	less
Burdick (D-N.D.)	68	16	61	—	more
Bentsen (D-Texas)	55	6	34	Rep.	less
Stafford (R-Vt.)	63	4	44	Gov.	more
Byrd (Ind.-Va.)	62	11	55	—	less
Jackson (D-Wash.)	64	18+	40	—	less
Byrd (D-W.Va.)	58	17	Unopposed		
Proxmire (D-Wis.)	60	18+	45	—	more
1978					
Stevens (R-Alaska)	54	10	61	—	less
Biden (D-Del.)	35	6	54	—	less
Nunn (D-Ga.)	40	6	53	—	less
McClure (R-Idaho)	50	6	43	—	less
Percy (R-Ill.)	59	12	44	—	less
Huddleston (D-Ky.)	52	6	34	—	less
Johnston (D-La.)	46	6	Unopposed		
Domenici (R-N.M.)	46	6	37	—	less
Helms (R-N.C.)	57	6	49	—	less

Table A-4 (Continued)

Incumbent	Age^1	Years in Senate[2]	Challenger		
			Age	Elective Office[3]	Spending[4]
Hatfield (R-Ore.)	56	12	53	—	less
Pell (D-R.I.)	59	18	35	—	less
Thurmond (R-S.C.)	75	18	40	—	less
Baker (R-Tenn.)	52	12	45	—	less
Tower (R-Texas)	53	17	43	Rep.	less
Randolph (D-W.Va.)	76	18	55	Gov.	less
1980					
Goldwater (R-Ariz.)	71	18+	49	—	more
Bumpers (D-Ark.)	55	6	37	—	less
Cranston (D-Calif.)	66	12	68	—	less
Hart (D-Colo.)	42	6	45	—	less
Inouye (D-Hawaii)	56	18	31	—	less
Dole (R-Kan.)	57	12	46	—	less
Ford (D-Ky.)	56	6	70	—	less
Long (D-La.)	61	18+	Unopposed		
Mathias (R-Md.)	58	12	51	—	less
Eagleton (D-Mo.)	51	12	45	—	less
Laxalt (R-Nev.)	58	6	44		less
Glenn (D-Ohio)	59	6	46	—	less
Packwood (R-Ore.)	48	12	39	—	less
Hollings (D-S.C.)	58	12	56	—	less
Garn (R-Utah)	48	6	45	—	less
Leahy (D-Vt.)	40	6	47	—	more

[1] Age is cited at the time of election.

[2] Senators running for a fifth or subsequent term are included together as serving more than 18 years in office.

[3] The elective office of the challenger includes service only as a present or former governor or U.S. representative or senator.

[4] "More" indicates that the challenger spent more than the incumbent. Data for 1974 were not available.

SOURCE: Collected by the author from Congressional Quarterly biographical information published in *Congressional Quarterly Weekly Reports* prior to each election. For information on 1976 and 1978 campaign receipts and expenditures see Appendix Table A-7. The 1980 spending comparisons were based on 1979-1980 gross expenditure figures provided by the Federal Election Commission.

NOTE: In 1980, two Senate incumbents were defeated by challengers who outspent them. Culver spent $1,750,680; his opponent $2,183,028. Morgan spent $948,209; his opponent $1,175,875. Two Senate incumbents in 1980 beat challengers who outspent them. Goldwater spent $949,992; his opponent $2,073,232. Leahy spent $434,644; his opponent $532,904.

Table A-5   House Incumbents Defeated, 1978, 1980

Incumbent	Terms Served	Percent of Vote in Preceding Election[1]	Total Spending[2]	Challenger's Increase in Spending[3]
1978				
McFall (D-Calif.)[4]	11	73	more	more
Krebs (D-Calif.)	2	66	more	more
Hannaford (D-Calif.)	2	51	less	less
Burke (R-Fla.)[4]	6	54	more	more
Cornwell (D-Ind.)	1	50	more	more
Blouin (D-Iowa)	2	51	more	more
Keys (D-Kan.)	2	52	more	more
Steers (R-Md.)	1	47	less	less
Brown (R-Mich.)	6	51	less	less
Cederberg (R-Mich.)	13	57	more	more
Meyner (D-N.J.)	2	51	more	more
Pattison (D-N.Y.)	2	47	more	more
Carney (D-Ohio)	4	51	less	less
Eilberg (D-Pa.)[4]	6	68	less	more
Rooney (D-Pa.)	8	65	less	more
Ammerman (D-Pa.)	1	57	more	more
Gammage (D-Tex.)	1	50	less	less[5]
Cunningham (R-Wash.)[6]	—	—	less	—
Cornell (D-Wis.)	2	52	more	more

Total: 19 defeated of 377 running for re-election

Incumbent	Terms Served	Percent of Vote in Preceding Election[1]	Total Spending[2]	Challenger's Increase in Spending[3]
1980				
Johnson (D-Calif.)	11	59	less	more
Royer (R-Calif.)[6]	—	—	less	—
Corman (D-Calif.)	10	59	less	less
Lloyd (D-Calif.)	3	54	more	more
Van Deerlin (D-Calif.)	9	74	more	more
Brademas (D-Ind.)	11	56	less	less
Leach (D-La.)	1	50	more	more
Bauman (R-Md.)[4]	3	64	less	less
Carr (D-Mich.)	3	57	more	more
Burlison (D-Mo.)	6	65	more	more
Thompson (D-N.J.)[4]	13	61	less	less
Maguire (D-N.J.)	3	53	more	more
Ambro (D-N.Y.)	3	51	more	more
Wolff (D-N.Y.)	8	60	more	more
Murphy (D-N.Y.)[4]	9	54	less	less
Preyer (D-N.C.)	6	68	more	more
Gudger (D-N.C.)	2	51	more	more
Ashley (D-Ohio)	13	63	more	more
Devine (R-Ohio)	11	57	more	more
Ullman (D-Ore.)	12	69	less	more

Table A-5   (Continued)

Incumbent	Terms Served	Percent of Vote in Preceding Election[1]	Total Spending[2]	Challenger's Increase in Spending[3]
Kostmayer (D-Pa.)	2	61	more	more
Musto (D-Pa.)[6]	—	—	less	—
Beard (D-R.I.)	3	53	more	more
Jenrette (D-S.C.)[4]	3	Unopposed	more	—
Eckhardt (D-Texas)	7	62	more	more
McKay (D-Utah)	5	51	less	less
Harris (D-Va.)	3	51	more	more
Fisher (D-Va.)	3	53	more	more
McCormack (D-Wash.)	5	61	more	more
Hutchinson (D-W.Va.)[6]	—	—	less	—
Baldus (D-Wis.)	3	63	more	more

Total: 31 defeated of 392 running for re-election

[1] The total vote percentages for the 1978 incumbents are from the 1976 election; the percentages for the 1980 incumbents are from the 1978 election.

[2] "More" indicates that the challenger spent more than the incumbent. In 1978, 11 challengers spent more, and 8 challengers spent less. In 1980, 20 challengers spent more, and 11 challengers spent less.

[3] "More" indicates that the challenger's increase in spending from 1976 to 1978 (or from 1978 to 1980) was greater than the increase in the incumbent's spending in the same period.

[4] Involved in a scandal before the election.

[5] The challenger Ron Raul set the 1976 record by spending $554,000. He spent $322,000 in 1978. (Gammage spent $250,000 and $477,000 in 1976 and 1978.) So while Paul's 1978 spending increase was less than the incumbent's, he spent the third highest amount of all of the victorious challengers. Only Martha Keys's and Helen Meyner's opponents spent more.

[6] Cunningham was elected during the 95th Congress. Royer, Musto, and Hutchinson were elected during the 96th Congress.

SOURCE: The list of defeated House incumbents in 1978 and 1980 was taken from *Congressional Quarterly Weekly Report*, November 11, 1978, p. 3250 and November 8, 1980, p. 3318. The 1976 percentage of the total vote and the information on 1976-1978 spending was supplied by Michael Barone et al., *The Almanac of American Politics 1980* (New York: E. P. Dutton, 1979). The total vote percentage for 1978 was supplied by *America Votes 13*, ed. Richard M. Scammon and Alice V. McGillivray (Washington, D.C.: Congressional Quarterly, 1979). The spending comparisons for 1980 incumbents and challengers were based on Federal Election Commission figures that reflect gross expenditures of candidates from 1979 to December 1980.

Table A-6 Funding Sources for Candidates in U.S. House and Senate General Elections, 1974-1978

Year	Amount Raised (In Millions of Dollars)	Individual Contributions $0-100	$101-499	$500+	Percent Distribution Nonparty PACs	Parties	Candidate to Self	Loans; Other	Total
House									
1974	45.7	(58% under $499)		15	17	4	6	—	(100%)
1976	65.7	37	12	11	23	8	9	1	(100%)
1978	92.2	35	10	12	25	7	9	2	(100%)
Senate									
1974	28.2	(49% under $499)		27	11	6	1	6	(100%)
1976	39.1	28	13	27	15	4	12	—	(100%)
1978	66.0	37	11	22	13	6	8	3	(100%)

SOURCE: Michael Malbin, "Of Mountains and Molehills: PACs, Campaigns, and Public Policy," in *Parties, Interest Groups, and Campaign Finance Laws*, ed. Michael Malbin (Washington, D.C.: American Enterprise Institute, 1980), pp. 154, 155. © 1980 by American Enterprise Institute.

Table A-7   Senate Campaign Spending, 1976, 1978 (In Dollars)

Candidates	Receipts	Expen-ditures	Cost Per Vote
1976 Senate Campaign			
ARIZONA			
Dennis DeConcini (D)	598,668	597,405	1.14
Sam Steiger (R)	722,691	679,384	1.60
CALIFORNIA			
John V. Tunney (D)*	1,903,527	1,940,988	0.37
S. I. Hayakawa (R)	1,218,485	1,184,624	0.26
CONNECTICUT			
Gloria Schaffer (D)	312,394	306,104	0.55
Lowell P. Weicker Jr. (R)*	500,955	480,709	0.61
DELAWARE			
Thomas C. Maloney (D)	211,281	211,258	2.15
William V. Roth Jr. (R)*	321,292	322,080	2.57
FLORIDA			
Lawton Chiles (D)*	362,477	362,235	0.20
John L. Grady (R)	408,616	394,574	0.13
HAWAII			
Spark M. Matsunaga (D)	416,775	435,130	1.62
William F. Quinn (R)	417,652	415,138	2.68
INDIANA			
Vance Hartke (D)*	662,389	654,279	0.55
Richard G. Lugar (R)	742,736	727,720	0.44
MAINE			
Edmund S. Muskie (D)*	322,964	320,427	1.09
Robert A. G. Monks (R)	602,851	598,490	2.13
MARYLAND			
Paul S. Sarbanes (D)	892,300	891,533	0.83
J. Glenn Beall (R)*	578,299	572,016	1.08
MASSACHUSETTS			
Edward M. Kennedy (D)*	975,601	896,196	0.40
Michael Robertson (R)	169,724	168,854	0.23
MICHIGAN			
Donald W. Riegle Jr. (D)	849,684	795,821	0.39
Marvin L. Esch (R)	864,759	809,564	0.47
MINNESOTA			
Hubert H. Humphrey (D)*	664,567	618,878	0.38
Gerald W. Brekke (R)	45,775	43,912	0.08
MISSISSIPPI			
John C. Stennis (D)*	119,852	119,852	0.17
MISSOURI			
Warren E. Hearnes (D)	662,737	660,953	0.63
John C. Danforth (R)	748,115	741,465	0.54
MONTANA			
John Melcher (D)	321,596	311,101	1.05
Stanley C. Burger (R)	578,826	563,543	3.82

NOTE: An asterisk (*) indicates an incumbent. The names of winners are italicized.

Table A-7   Senate Campaign Spending, 1976, 1978 (In Dollars)

Candidates	Receipts	Expenditures	Cost Per Vote
1976 Senate Campaign (Cont.)			
NEBRASKA			
Edward Zorinsky (D)	240,904	237,613	0.60
John Y. McCollister (R)	391,289	391,287	0.90
NEVADA			
Howard W. Cannon (D)*	422,203	405,380	2.15
David Towell (R)	58,842	58,842	0.66
NEW JERSEY			
Harrison A. Williams Jr. (D)*	690,781	610,090	0.30
David F. Norcross (R)	74,023	73,499	0.59
NEW MEXICO			
Joseph M. Montoya (D)*	461,505	451,111	1.66
Harrison H. Schmitt (R)	473,336	441,309	1.64
NEW YORK			
Daniel Patrick Moynihan (D)	1,219,740	1,210,796	0.32
James L. Buckley (Cons R)*	2,090,126	2,101,424	0.68
NORTH DAKOTA			
Quentin N. Burdick (D)*	122,605	117,514	0.67
Robert Stroup (R)	142,774	136,748	1.32
OHIO			
Howard M. Metzenbaum (D)	1,097,337	1,092,053	0.43
Robert Taft Jr. (R)*	1,328,283	1,304,207	0.72
PENNSYLVANIA			
William J. Green (D)	1,266,375	1,269,409	0.44
H. John Heinz III (R)	3,016,731	3,004,814	1.10
RHODE ISLAND			
Richard P. Lorber (D)	782,663	782,931	3.44
John H. Chafee (R)	424,463	415,651	1.80
TENNESSEE			
James R. Sasser (D)	841,644	839,379	0.84
Bill Brock (R)*	1,313,503	1,301,033	1.93
TEXAS			
Lloyd Bentsen (D)*	1,277,364	1,237,910	0.39
Alan Steelman (R)	667.214	665,058	0.35
UTAH			
Frank E. Moss (D)*	365,187	343,598	1.42
Orrin G. Hatch (R)	393,278	370,517	0.94
VERMONT			
Thomas P. Salmon (D)	170,156	169,296	1.98
Robert T. Stafford (R)*	167,469	157,927	1.67
VIRGINIA			
Elmo R. Zumwalt Jr. (D)	450,229	443,107	0.74
Harry F. Byrd Jr. (Ind.)*	809,346	802,928	0.90
WASHINGTON			
Henry M. Jackson (D)*	223,322	198,375	0.12
George M. Brown (R)	10,841	10,841	0.03

NOTE: An asterisk (*) indicates an incumbent. The names of winners are italicized.

Table A-7 (Continued)

Candidates	Receipts	Expen-ditures	Cost Per Vote
WEST VIRGINIA			
Robert C. Byrd (D)*	271,124	94,335	0.17
WISCONSIN			
William Proxmire (D)*	25	697	0.00
Stanley York (R)	66,321	62,210	0.12
WYOMING			
Gale W. McGee (D)*	299,908	181,028	2.57
Malcolm Wallop (R)	305,161	301,595	2.39

1978 Senate Campaign

ALABAMA			
Howell Heflin (D)	1,107,015	1,059,113	0.76
Donald Stewart (D)	823,619	816,456	0.71
James D. Martin (R)	539,267	552,504	1.75
ALASKA			
Donald W. Hobbs (D)	15,527	21,234	0.53
Ted Stevens (R)*	366,895	346,837	3.74
ARKANSAS			
David Pryor (D)	802,861	774,824	0.90
Thomas Kelly Jr. (R)	16,210	16,208	0.19
COLORADO			
Floyd K. Haskell (D)*	658,657	664,249	2.01
William L. Armstrong (R)	1,163,790	1,081,944	1.84
DELAWARE			
Joseph R. Biden Jr. (D)	487,637	487,504	5.19
James H. Baxter (R)	207,637	206,250	2.62
GEORGIA			
Sam Nunn (D)*	708,417	548,814	0.52
John W. Stokes (R)	7,291	6,640	0.05
IDAHO			
Dwight Jensen (D)	55,163	55,163	0.62
James A. McClure (R)*	378,084	385,536	1.98
ILLINOIS			
Alex R. Seith (D)	1,370,457	1,371,185	0.57
Charles H. Percy (R)*	2,185,153	2,163,555	1.03
IOWA			
Dick Clark (D)*	862,635	860,774	1.78
Roger Jepsen (R)	738,581	728,268	1.43
KANSAS			
Bill Roy (D)	824,537	813,754	1.95
Nancy Landon Kassebaum (R)	864,288	856,644	1.82
KENTUCKY			
Walter (Dee) Huddleston (D)*	395,557	456,432	1.20
Louie R. Guenthner (R)	77,012	76,445	0.40

NOTE: An asterisk (*) indicates an incumbent. The names of winners are italicized.

Table A-7 Senate Campaign Spending, 1976, 1978 (In Dollars)

Candidates	Receipts	Expen-ditures	Cost Per Vote
1978 Senate Campaign (Cont.)			
LOUISIANA			
J. Bennett Johnston Jr. (D)*	983,343	857,860	1.72
MAINE			
William D. Hathaway (D)*	423,499	423,027	3.32
William S. Cohen (R)	658,254	648,739	3.06
MASSACHUSETTS			
Paul E. Tsongas (D)	772,513	768,383	0.55
Edward W. Brooke (R)*	957,252	1,284,855	1.24
MICHIGAN			
Carl Levin (D)	994,439	971,775	0.57
Robert P. Griffin (R)*	1,691,534	1,681,550	1.00
MINNESOTA			
Wendell R. Anderson (D)*	1,155,562	1,154,351	1.25
Rudy Boschwitz (R)	1,902,861	1,870,163	1.73
Robert E. Short (D)	1,982,442	1,972,060	2.48
David Durenberger (R)	1,073,135	1,062,271	0.97
MISSISSIPPI			
Maurice Dantin (D)	874,590	873,518	1.67
Thad Cochran (R)	1,201,259	1,052,303	3.35
Charles Evers (I)	142,684	135,119	1.01
MONTANA			
Max Baucus (D)	668,189	653,756	2.64
Larry Williams (R)	352,848	346,721	2.13
NEBRASKA			
J. J. Exon (D)	262,404	234,862	0.70
Donald E. Shasteen (R)	222,190	218,148	0.76
NEW HAMPSHIRE			
Thomas J. McIntyre (D)*	298,608	289,628	1.81
Gordon Humphrey (R)	366,632	357,107	2.11
NEW JERSEY			
Bill Bradley (D)	1,689,975	1,688,499	1.30
Jeffrey Bell (R)	1,432,924	1,418,931	1.47
NEW MEXICO			
Toney Anaya (D)	175,659	175,633	1.10
Pete V. Domenici (R)*	925,622	914,634	4.99
NORTH CAROLINA			
John R. Ingram (D)	261,982	264,088	0.26
Jesse Helms (R)*	7,463,282	7,460,966	12.05
OKLAHOMA			
David L. Boren (D)	779,544	751,286	0.73
Robert Kamm (R)	444,734	443,712	1.79
OREGON			
Vern Cook (D)	38,977	38,976	0.08
Mark O. Hatfield (R)*	277,059	223,874	0.32

NOTE: An asterisk (*) indicates an incumbent. The names of winners are italicized.

Table A-7   (Continued)

Candidates	Receipts	Expenditures	Cost Per Vote
RHODE ISLAND			
Claiborne Pell (D)*	398,898	373,077	1.25
James G. Reynolds (R)	85,615	85,614	1.13
SOUTH CAROLINA			
Charles D.			
(Pug) Ravenel (D)	1,145,542	1,134,168	2.33
Strom Thurmond (R)*	1,753,628	2,013,431	5.72
SOUTH DAKOTA			
Don Barnett (D)	152,665	152,006	1.25
Larry Pressler (R)	489,983	449,541	1.89
TENNESSEE			
Jane Eskind (D)	1,906,603	1,903,532	3.00
Howard H.			
Baker Jr. (R)*	1,946,071	1,922,573	2.27
TEXAS			
Robert (Bob) Krueger (D)	2,431,204	2,428,666	1.22
John G. Tower (R)*	4,264,015	4,324,601	3.76
VIRGINIA			
Andrew P. Miller (D)	850,313	832,773	1.37
John W. Warner (R)	2,907,073	2,897,237	4.72
WEST VIRGINIA			
Jennings Randolph (D)*	732,484	684,605	1.59
Arch A. Moore Jr. (R)	474,218	458,823	1.37
WYOMING			
Raymond B. Whitaker (D)	143,051	142,749	2.03
Alan K. Simpson (R)	442,484	439,805	3.66

SOURCE: The figures on receipts and expenditures were compiled by the Federal Election Commission. The cost per vote was compiled by Congressional Quarterly. Cost per vote includes votes cast in contested primaries, runoffs, and the general election. Receipt and expenditure figures include repaid loans but exclude transfers to and from affiliated committees. This list includes only candidates in the general election who received 10% or more of the vote.

NOTE: An asterisk (*) indicates an incumbent. The names of winners are italicized.

Table A-8   Women in the House of Representatives

	1974 % Total Vote	1976 % Total Vote	1978 % Total Vote	1980 % Total Vote
Incumbents				
Sullivan (D-Mo.)	75.3	Retired	—	—
Schroeder (D-Colo.)	58.5	53.2	61.5	59.8
Mink (D-Hawaii)	62.6	Retired	—	—
Jordan (D-Texas)	84.8	85.5	Retired	—
Holtzman (D-N.Y.)	78.9	82.9	81.9	Ran for Senate
Collins (D-Ill.)	87.9	84.8	86.3	85.1
Chisholm (D-N.Y.)	80.2	87.0	87.8	87.1
Brathwaite (D-Calif.)	80.1	80.2	Retired	—
Boggs (D-La.)	81.8	92.6	100.0	60.8
Abzug (D-N.Y.)	78.7	Retired	—	—
Holt (R-Md.)	58.1	57.7	62.0	71.9
Heckler (R-Mass.)	64.2	100.0	61.1	60.6
Nonincumbents				
1974				
Keys (D-Kan.)	55.0†	50.7	48.0	—
(Lloyd) Bouquard (D-Tenn.)	51.1*	67.5	88.9	61.1
Meyner (D-N.J.)	57.3*	50.4	48.2	—
Spellman (D-Md.)	52.6†	57.7	77.2	80.5#
Fenwick (R-N.J.)	53.4†	66.9	72.6	75.7
Smith (R-Neb.)	50.2†	72.9	80.0	83.9
1976				
Oakar (D-Ohio)	—	81.0†	100.0	100.0
Mikulski (D-Md.)	—	74.6†	100.0	76.1
1978				
Byron (D-Md.)	—	—	89.7†	69.9
Ferraro (D-N.Y.)	—	—	54.2†	58.3
Snowe (R-Maine)	—	—	50.8†	78.5
1980				
Fiedler (R-Calif.)	—	—	—	48.7*
Martin (R-Ill.)	—	—	—	50.8†
Roukema (R-N.J.)	—	—	—	50.7*
Schneider (R-R.I.)	—	—	—	55.3*

† A dagger indicates the candidate ran in an open-seat contest.

* An asterisk indicates the candidate ran against an incumbent.

The 5th District of Maryland seat held by Gladys Noon Spellman (D) was declared vacant by the House February 24, 1981.

SOURCE: *America Votes 13*, ed. Richard M. Scammon and Alice V. McGillivray (Washington, D.C.: Congressional Quarterly, 1979). The 1980 percentages of the total vote were based on final official vote totals submitted by the states.

NOTE: The percentages of the total vote reflect electoral victories, with only two exceptions. In 1978, Martha Keys, who received 48.0% of the total vote, and Helen Meyner, who received 48.2% of the total vote, were both defeated.

Table A-9 Terms of Service in the House and Senate, 1953-1980

	CONGRESS													
	83rd	84th	85th	86th	87th	88th	89th	90th	91st	92nd	93rd	94th	95th	96th
Percent of Representatives Serving														
1-2 terms	32	29	20	28	28	28	33	29	23	21	27	34	36	32
3-9 terms	57	58	64	57	55	56	51	53	60	58	56	53	51	56
10+ terms	10	12	16	15	17	17	17	17	18	20	18	14	14	13
Total %	99	99	100	100	100	101	101	99	101	99	101	101	101	101
Number of Senators Serving														
1 term or less	38	43	36	41	42	44	29	28	31	27	40	35	43	48
2-3 terms	52	47	51	47	49	47	53	54	52	58	42	49	42	36
more than 3 terms	6	6	9	10	9	9	18	18	17	15	18	15	15	16
Total No.	96	96	96	98	100	100	100	100	100	100	100	99	100	100

SOURCE: John Bibby et al., *Vital Statistics on Congress, 1980* (Washington, D.C.: American Enterprise Institute, 1980), pp. 53, 54. © 1980 by American Enterprise Institute.

Bibliography

Studies of Congressional Elections

This bibliography is an attempt to compile a comprehensive listing of the literature on congressional elections, from the late 1960s to early 1981, in books by political scientists and articles in political science journals.

Abramowitz, A. "Choices and Echoes in the 1978 U. S. Senate Elections: A Research Note." *American Journal of Political Science* (February 1981): 112-118.

———. "A Comparison of Voting for U.S. Senator and Representative in 1978." *American Political Science Review* (September 1980): 633-640.

———. "Name Familiarity, Reputation, and the Incumbency Effect in a Congressional Election." *Western Political Quarterly* (December 1975): 668-684.

Arcelus, F., and Meltzer, A. H. "The Effect of Aggregate Economic Variables on Congressional Elections." *American Political Science Review* (December 1975): 1232-1239. See also the comments on pp. 1255-1266.

Arseneau, R., and Wolfinger, R. "Voting Behavior in Congressional Elections." Paper presented at the annual meeting of the American Political Science Association, New Orleans, Louisiana, September 4-8, 1973.

Bloom, H., and Price, H. "Voter Response to Short Run Economic Conditions: The Asymmetric Effect of Prosperity and Recession." *American Political Science Review* (December 1975): 1240-1254.

Born, R. "Changes in the Competitiveness of House Primary Elections, 1956-1976." *American Politics Quarterly* (October 1980): 495-506.

———. "House Incumbents and Inter-Election Vote Change." *Journal of Politics* (1977): 1008-1034.

Buck, J. V. "Presidential Coattails and Congressional Loyalty." *Midwest Journal of Political Science* (August 1972): 460-472.

Burnham, W. D. "Insulation and Responsiveness in Congressional Elections." *Political Science Quarterly* (Fall 1975): 411-435.

Clem, Alan L., ed. *The Making of Congressmen: Seven Campaigns of 1974.* North Scituate, Mass.: Duxbury Press, 1976.

Conway, M., and Wyckoff, M. "Voter Choice in the 1974 Congressional Elections. *American Politics Quarterly* (January 1980): 3-14.

Cook, T. "Legislature vs. Legislator: A Note on the Paradox of Congressional Support." *Legislative Studies Quarterly* (February 1979): 43-52.

Cover, A. "One Good Term Deserves Another: The Advantage of Incumbency in Congressional Elections." *American Journal of Political Science* (August 1977): 523-542.

Cover, A., and Mayhew, D. "Congressional Dynamics and the Decline of Competitive Congressional Elections." In *Congress Reconsidered*, 2nd ed., edited by L. Dodd and B. Oppenheimer, pp. 62-82. Washington, D.C.: Congressional Quarterly, 1981.

Cowart, A. "Electoral Choice in the American States." *American Political Science Review* (September 1973): 835-853.

Cummings, M. *Congressmen and the Electorate.* New York: Free Press, 1966.

Darcy, R., and Schramm, S. "When Women Run Against Men." *Public Opinion Quarterly* (1977): 1-12.

Dawson, P., and Zinser, J. "Broadcast Expenditures and Electoral Outcomes in the 1970 Congressional Elections." *Public Opinion Quarterly* (Fall 1970): 398-402.

_____. "Characteristics of Campaign Resource Allocation in the 1972 Congressional Elections." In *Changing Campaign Techniques*, edited by L. Maisel, Sage Electoral Studies Yearbook, vol. 2, pp. 93-138. Beverly Hills: Sage Publications, 1976.

Edwards, G. "The Impact of Presidential Coattails on Outcomes of Congressional Elections." *American Politics Quarterly* (January 1979): 94-108.

Erikson, R. "The Advantage of Incumbency in Congressional Elections." *Polity* (Spring 1971): 395-405.

_____. "Constituency Opinion and Congressional Behavior." *American Journal of Political Science* (August 1978): 511-535.

_____. "The Electoral Impact of Congressional Roll Call Voting." *American Political Science Review* (December 1971): 1018-1032.

_____. "Is There Such a Thing as a Safe Seat?" *Polity* (Summer 1976): 623-632.

_____. "Malapportionment, Gerrymandering, and Party Fortunes in Congressional Elections." *American Political Science Review* (December 1972): 1234-1245.

Erikson, R., and Wright, G. "Policy Representation of Constituency Interests." *Political Behavior* 1 (1980): 91-106.

Fenno, R. *Home Style.* Boston: Little, Brown & Co., 1978.

_____. "If, As Ralph Nader Says, Congress is 'The Broken Branch,' How Come We Love Our Congressmen So Much?" In *Congress in Change*, edited by N. Ornstein, pp. 277-287. New York: Praeger Publishers, 1975.

_____. "U.S. House Members in Their Constituencies." *American Political Science Review* (September 1977): 883-917.

Ferejohn, J. "On the Decline of Competition in Congressional Elections." *American Political Science Review* (March 1977): 166-176.

Fiorina, M. "The Case of the Vanishing Marginals: The Bureaucracy Did It." *American Political Science Review* (March 1977): 177-181.

_____. "Electoral Margins, Constituency Influence, and Policy Moderation." *American Politics Quarterly* (October 1973): 479-498.

Fowler, L. "Candidate Perceptions of Electoral Coalitions." *American Politics Quarterly* (October 1980): 483-494.

Glantz, S., et al. "Election Outcomes: Whose Money Matters." *Journal of Politics* (November 1976): 1033-1041.

Goldenberg, E., and Traugott, M. "Campaign Effects on Outcomes in the 1978 Congressional Elections." Paper presented at the Houston-Rice Conference on Congressional Elections Research, Houston, Texas, January 1980.

_____. "Congressional Campaign Effects on Candidate Recognition and Evaluation." *Political Behavior* 1 (1980): 61-90.

Hershey, M. "Incumbency and the Minimum Winning Coalition." *American Journal of Political Science* (August 1973): 631-637.

Hinckley, B. "The American Voter in Congressional Elections." *American Political Science Review* (September 1980): 641-650.

_____. "House Reelections and Senate Defeats: The Role of the Challenger." *British Journal of Political Science* (October 1980): 441-460.

_____. "Incumbency and the Presidential Vote in Senate Elections." *American Political Science Review* (September 1970): 628-642.

_____. "Interpreting House Midterm Elections." *American Political Science Review* (September 1967): 694-700.

_____. "Issues, Information Costs, and Congressional Elections." *American Politics Quarterly* (April 1976): 131-152.

Hinckley, B., Hofstetter, R., and Kessel, J. "Information and the Vote: A Comparative Election Study." *American Politics Quarterly* (April 1974): 131-158.

Hurley, P., and Hill, K. "The Prospects for Issue-Voting in Contemporary Elections." *American Politics Quarterly* (October 1980): 425-448.

Jacobson, G. "The Effects of Campaign Spending on Congressional Elections." *American Political Science Review* (June 1978): 469-491.

_____. "The Impact of Broadcast Campaigning on Electoral Outcomes." *Journal of Politics* (August 1975): 769-793.

_____. "Incumbents and Voters in the 1978 Congressional Elections." *Legislative Studies Quarterly* (May 1981).

_____. *Money in Congressional Elections.* New Haven: Yale University Press, 1980.

_____. "Presidential Coattails in 1972." *Public Opinion Quarterly* (Summer 1976): 194-200.

Jones, C. *Every Second Year.* Washington, D.C.: Brookings Institution, 1967.

_____. "The Role of the Campaign in Congressional Politics." In *The Electoral Process,* edited by M. K. Jennings and L. H. Zeigler, pp. 21-41. Englewood Cliffs, N. J.: Prentice-Hall, 1966.

Kabaker, H. "Estimating the Normal Vote in Congressional Elections." *Midwest Journal of Political Science* (February 1969): 58-83.

Kaplowitz, S. "Using Aggregate Voting Data to Measure Presidential Coattail Effects." *Public Opinion Quarterly* (Fall 1971): 415-419.

Kernell, S. "Presidential Popularity and Negative Voting." *American Political Science Review* (March 1977): 44-66.

Kinder, D., and Kiewiet, D. "Economic Discontent and Political Behavior." *American Journal of Political Science* (August 1979): 495-527.

Kingdon, J. *Candidates for Office: Beliefs and Strategies.* New York: Random House, 1966.

Kostroski, W. "Party and Incumbency in Postwar Senate Elections." *American Political Science Review* (December 1973): 1213-1234.

Kritzer, H., and Eubank, R. "Presidential Coattails Revisited: Partisanship and Incumbency Effects." *American Journal of Political Science* (August 1979): 616-625.

Kuklinski, J., and West, D. "Economic Expectations and Mass Voting in United States House and Senate Elections." *American Political Science Review* (June 1981).

Li, R. "Dynamic Comparative Analysis of Presidential and House Elections." *American Journal of Political Science* (November 1976): 671-691.

Maisel, L. "Congressional Elections in 1978: The Road to Nomination, The Road to Election." *American Politics Quarterly* (January 1981): 23-48.

Maisel, L., and Cooper, J., eds. *Sage Electoral Studies Yearbook*, vol. 6. Beverly Hills: Sage Publications, 1981.

Mann, T. *Unsafe At Any Margin*. Washington, D.C.: American Enterprise Institute, 1978.

Mann, T., and Wolfinger, R. "Candidates and Parties in Congressional Elections." *American Political Science Review* (September 1980): 617-632.

Mayhew, D. *Congress: The Electoral Connection*. New Haven: Yale University Press, 1974.

———. "Congressional Elections: The Case of the Vanishing Marginals." *Polity* (Spring 1974): 295-317.

McLeod, J., et al. "Watergate and the 1974 Congressional Elections." *Public Opinion Quarterly* (Summer 1977): 181-195.

Miller, W., and Stokes, D. "Constituency Influence in Congress." *American Political Science Review* (March 1963): 45-57.

Moreland, W. "Angels, Pinpoints and Voters: The Pattern for a Coattail." *American Journal of Political Science* (February 1973): 170-176.

Nelson, C. "The Effect of Incumbency on Voting in Congressional Elections." *Political Science Quarterly* (Winter 1978/1979): 665-678.

Owens, J., and Olson, E. "Economic Fluctuations and Congressional Elections." *American Journal of Political Science* (August 1980): 469-493.

Parker, G. "The Advantage of Incumbency in House Elections." *American Politics Quarterly* (October 1980): 449-464.

———. "The Impact of Short-Term Forces in Congressional Election Preferences: 1941-1978." Paper presented at the Project 87 Conference, Washington, D.C., February 1981.

Parker, G., and Davidson, R. "Why Do Americans Love their Congressmen So Much More than their Congress?" *Legislative Studies Quarterly* (February 1979): 53-62.

Patterson, S., et al. *Representatives and Represented*. New York: John Wiley & Sons, 1975.

Payne, J. "The Personal Electoral Advantage of House Incumbents, 1936-1976." *American Politics Quarterly* (October 1980): 465-482.

Peters, J., and Welch, S. "The Effects of Charges of Corruption on Voting Behavior in Congressional Elections." *American Political Science Review* (September 1980): 697-708.

Piereson, J. "Presidential Popularity and Midterm Voting at Different Election Levels." *American Journal of Political Science* (November 1975): 683-694.

Ragsdale, L. "The Fiction of Congressional Elections as Presidential Events." *American Politics Quarterly* (October 1980): 375-398.

———. "Incumbent Popularity, Challenger Invisibility, and Congressional Voters." *Legislative Studies Quarterly* (May 1981): 201-218.

Schantz, H. "Contested and Uncontested Primaries for the U.S. House." *Legislative Studies Quarterly* (November 1980): 545-562.

Schoenberger, R. "Campaign Strategy and Party Loyalty: The Electoral Relevance of Candidate Decision-Making in the 1964 Congressional Elections." *American Political Science Review* (June 1969): 515-520.

Shannon, W. "Electoral Margins and Voting Behavior in the House of Representatives." *Journal of Politics* (November 1968): 1028-1045.
Stokes, D., and Miller, W. "Party Government and the Salience of Congress." *Public Opinion Quarterly* (Winter 1962): 531-546.
Stone, W. "The Dynamics of Constituency Electoral Control in the House." *American Politics Quarterly* (October 1980): 399-424.
Sullivan, J., and Minns, D. "Ideological Distance Between Candidates." *American Journal of Political Science* (August 1976): 439-468.
Sullivan, J., and Uslaner, E. "Congressional Behavior and Election Marginality." *American Journal of Political Science* (August 1978): 536-553.
Tufte, E. "Determinants of the Outcome of Midterm Congressional Elections." *American Political Science Review* (September 1975): 812-826.
Uslaner, E. " 'Ain't Misbehavin': The Logic of Defensive Issue Strategies in Congressional Elections." *American Politics Quarterly* (January 1981): 3-22.
Weissberg, R. "Collective and Dyadic Representation in Congress." *American Political Science Review* (June 1978): 535-547.
Wright, G. "Candidates' Policy Position and Voting in U.S. Congressional Elections." *Legislative Studies Quarterly* (August 1978): 445-464.
_____. "Constituency Response to Congressional Behavior: The Impact of the House Judiciary Committee Impeachment Votes." *Western Political Quarterly* (September 1977): 401-410.
_____. *Electoral Choice in America.* Chapel Hill: Institute for Research in Social Science, 1974.
Zeidenstein, H. "Measuring Congressional Seat Losses." *Journal of Politics* (February 1972): 272-276.

Other Election Studies

This is a selected list of studies outside the congressional literature that should be useful to all students of elections.

Achen, C. "Mass Political Attitudes and the Survey Response." *American Political Science Review* (December 1975): 1218-1231.
Asher, H. *Presidential Elections and American Politics*, 2nd ed. Homewood, Ill.: Dorsey Press, 1980.
Axelrod, R. "Where the Votes Come From: An Analysis of Electoral Coalitions, 1952-1968." *American Political Science Review* (March 1972): 11-20.
Bishop, G., et al. "Change in the Structure of American Political Attitudes." *American Journal of Political Science* (May 1978). See also comments in February 1979 issue, pp. 139-193.
_____. "Changing Structure of Mass Belief Systems." *Journal of Politics* (August 1978): 781-790.
Boyd, R. "Popular Control of Public Policy: A Normal Vote Analysis of the 1968 Election." *American Political Science Review* (June 1972): 429-449.
Brody, R., and Page, B. "Indifference, Alienation, and Rational Decisions: The Effects of Candidate Evaluations on Turnout and the Vote." *Public Choice* (Summer 1973): 1-19.
_____. "Policy Voting and the Electoral Process: The Vietnam War Issue." *American Political Science Review* (September 1972): 979-995.
Burnham, W. D. *Critical Elections and the Mainsprings of American Politics.* New York: W. W. Norton & Co., 1970.

Campbell, A. "Surge and Decline: A Study of Electoral Change." In *Elections and the Political Order,* edited by Campbell et al., pp. 40-62. New York: John Wiley & Sons, 1966.

Campbell, A., et al. *The American Voter.* New York: John Wiley & Sons, 1960.

Converse, P. "The Concept of the Normal Vote." In *Elections and the Political Order,* edited by Campbell et al., pp. 9-39. New York: John Wiley & Sons, 1966.

_____. "The Nature of Belief Systems." In *Ideology and Discontent,* edited by D. Apter, pp. 206-261. New York: Free Press, 1964.

Dennis, J. "Support for the Institution of Elections by the Mass Public." *American Political Science Review* (September 1970): 819-835.

Downs, A. *An Economic Theory of Democracy.* New York: Harper & Row, 1957.

Ferejohn, J., and Fiorina, M. "The Paradox of Not Voting: A Decision Theoretic Analysis. *American Political Science Review* (June 1970): 426-446.

Goldberg, A. "Discerning a Causal Pattern Among Data on Voting Behavior." *American Political Science Review* (December 1966): 913-922.

Kelley, S., Jr., and Mirer, T. "The Simple Act of Voting." *American Political Science Review* (June 1974): 572-591.

Kessel, J. *Presidential Campaign Politics: Coalition Strategies and Citizen Representation.* Homewood, Ill.: Dorsey Press, 1980.

Key, V. O., Jr. *The Responsible Electorate.* New York: Vintage Books, 1966.

Knoke, D. "A Causal Synthesis of Sociological and Psychological Models of American Voting Behavior." *Social Forces* (September 1974): 92-101.

Kramer, G. "Short Term Fluctuations in U.S. Voting Behavior: 1896-1964." *American Political Science Review* (March 1971): 131-143.

Lewis-Beck, M. "Evaluating the Effects of Independent Variables." *Political Methodology* (1976): 27-48.

Malbin, M., ed. *Parties, Interest Groups, and Campaign Finance Laws.* Washington, D.C.: American Enterprise Institute, 1980.

Margolis, M. "From Confusion to Confusion: Issues and the American Voter (1956-1972)." *American Political Science Review* (March 1977): 31-43.

Meier, K., and Campbell, J. "Issue Voting: An Empirical Examination of Individually Necessary and Jointly Sufficient Conditions." *American Politics Quarterly* (January 1979): 21-50.

Miller, A. "Normal Vote Analysis: Sensitivity to Change Over Time." *American Journal of Political Science* (May 1979): 406-425.

Miller, A., et al. "A Majority Party in Disarray." *American Political Science Review* (September 1976): 753-778, and other comments in this issue.

Miller, W., et al. *American National Election Studies Data Sourcebook: 1952-1978.* Cambridge: Harvard University Press, 1980.

Nie, N., and Andersen, K. "Mass Belief Systems Revisited." *Journal of Politics* (August 1974): 540-587.

Nie, N., et al. *The Changing American Voter.* Cambridge: Harvard University Press, 1976.

Niemi, R., and Weisberg, H., eds. *Controversies in American Voting Behavior.* San Francisco: W. H. Freeman & Co., 1976.

Page, B. *Choices and Echoes in Presidential Elections.* Chicago: University of Chicago Press, 1978.

Petrocik, J. "An Analysis of Intransitives in the Index of Party Identification." *Political Methodology* (Summer 1974): 31-47.

Pierce, J., and Sullivan, J., eds. *The Electorate Reconsidered.* Beverly Hills: Sage Publications, 1980.

Pomper, G. "From Confusion to Clarity: Issues and American Voters, 1956-1965." *American Political Science Review* (June 1972): 415-428.

RePass, D. "Issue Salience and Party Choice." *American Political Science Review* (June 1971): 389-400.

Riker, W., and Ordeshook, P. "A Theory of the Calculus of Voting." *American Political Science Review* (March 1968): 25-42.

Schulman, M., and Pomper, G. "Variability in Electoral Behavior: Longitudinal Perspectives from Causal Modeling." *American Journal of Political Science* (February 1975): 1-18.

Shapiro, M. "Rational Political Man: A Synthesis of Economic and Psychological Perspectives." *American Political Science Review* (December 1969): 1106-1119.

Shively, W. "The Development of Party Identification in Adults." *American Political Science Review* (December 1979): 1039-1054.

Stimson, J. "Belief Systems: Constraint, Complexity, and the 1972 Elections." *American Journal of Political Science* (August 1975): 393-417.

Stokes, D. "Some Dynamic Elements of Contests for the Presidency." *American Political Science Review* (March 1966): 19-28.

_____. "Spatial Models of Party Competition." *American Political Science Review* (June 1963): 368-377.

Sullivan, J., et al. "Ideological Constraint in the Mass Public: A Methodological Critique and Some New Findings." *American Journal of Political Science* (May 1978): 233-249. See also comments in the February 1979 issue, pp. 139-193.

Verba, S., and Nie, N. *Participation in America.* New York: Harper & Row, 1972.

Weisberg, H. "A Multidimensional Conceptualization of Party Identification." *Political Behavior* 1(1980): 33-60.

Weisberg, H., and Rusk, J. "Dimensions of Candidate Evaluation." *American Political Science Review* (December 1970): 1167-1185.

Wolfinger, R., and Rosenstone, S. *Who Votes?* New Haven: Yale University Press, 1980.

Index